W9-AEJ-755

Columbia University

*STUDIES IN CLASSICAL PHILOLOGY*

# COSTUME IN ROMAN COMEDY

# COSTUME IN ROMAN COMEDY

BY

CATHARINE SAUNDERS, Ph.D.

INSTRUCTOR IN LATIN, VASSAR COLLEGE

New York
THE COLUMBIA UNIVERSITY PRESS
1909

Set up and electrotyped. Published June, 1909.

Norwood Press
J. S. Cushing Co. — Berwick & Smith Co.
Norwood, Mass., U.S.A.

## PREFATORY NOTE

THIS monograph contains, in most convenient form, a mass of evidence concerning Costume in Roman Comedy nowhere else accessible. Dr. Saunders has done a real service to the student of the Roman theatre in gathering together all that our extant comedies have to teach us on this subject, in comparing or contrasting with this evidence that afforded by frescoes and reliefs at Pompeii and elsewhere, and in describing more minutely than has been done before, the costumes represented by the Terentian miniatures. Her work on the miniatures, aside from its direct relation to the immediate theme of her monograph, constitutes an important contribution to the discussion of the vexed question of the date of the miniatures, and goes far of itself to disprove the extravagant beliefs once held in their extreme antiquity.

HARRY THURSTON PECK.

COLUMBIA UNIVERSITY,
June 1, 1909.

# PREFACE

THE following study of Costume in Roman Comedy was suggested by the absence of any complete treatment of the subject, either in special dissertations or in those manuals of Roman life and customs which include an account of the Roman theatre. Further justification for such a study lies in the recent accession of certain material which had never before been available in reliable form, and, at the same time, in sufficient quantity. I refer to the photographic reproduction of miniatures from seven manuscripts of Terence, published at Leyden in 1903.[1]

The period for which I have sought to collect evidence is especially that of Plautus and Terence, but, for obvious reasons, I have also included much that may have belonged only to a later time.

I have given to the term *costume* a broad meaning, including under it not only the actual dress of the actors, but also such other properties as have

[1] Terenti Codex Ambrosianus H 75 inf. phototypice editus. Praefatus est Ericus Bethe. Accedunt 91 imagines ex aliis Terenti codicibus et libris impressis nunc primum collectae et editae. Lugduni Batavorum (A. W. Sijthoff), 1903.

a particularly close connection with the characters under discussion.

It was originally my intention to consider the problem of masks along with that of costume. However, a mere summary of the literature of this question was hardly justifiable; on the other hand, it soon became evident that a thorough and independent investigation of the subject must be postponed, since the material involved is quite sufficient to form the basis of a separate monograph.

I desire to take this opportunity to express my gratitude to those members of the Division of Classical Philology in Columbia University under whom I have studied — to Professors Perry, Wheeler, Egbert, McCrea, Lodge, Young, Knapp, and Olcott. In connection with this dissertation, my thanks are due to Professor Lodge for allowing me to consult the unpublished collections for his Lexicon Plautinum and, especially, to Professor Knapp, at whose suggestion this investigation was undertaken and under whose direction it was pursued, to whose wide knowledge of Roman comedy I have constantly appealed, and to whose scholarly criticism throughout the work I am deeply indebted.

CATHARINE SAUNDERS.

VASSAR COLLEGE,
April 17, 1909.

# CONTENTS

# COSTUME IN ROMAN COMEDY

## CHAPTER I

### SOURCES

In the detailed discussion of Costume in Roman Comedy I have taken into account the evidence furnished by two classes of material — the one literary, the other artistic. Under the literary evidence are included:

(1) The comedies of Plautus and Terence.[1]

(2) References to the stage in Donatus and Euanthius, including the commentary of Donatus on Terence and, more especially, the treatise known as De Comoedia.

(3) References to the stage in the Onomasticon of Pollux, particularly those chapters from Book IV which deal with costume

[1] I have not considered the Fragmenta of Plautus and the other comic writers. Since fragments are notoriously difficult of interpretation, it seemed wiser to restrict my references to complete dramas. I have used, almost without exception, the Teubner texts of Plautus and Terence.

(115–120) and with the masks used in comedy (143–154).

(4) Scattered references, mainly from Roman literature.

Under the artistic evidence are included:

(1) The illustrated manuscripts of Terence.[1]
(2) Pompeian wall-paintings.[2]
(3) Campanian reliefs.[3]

---

[1] For the reproductions of miniatures which I have consulted see Bibliography, pp. 143–144. I have not had access to the following famous works, which contain more or less inaccurate reproductions of miniatures from one of the best illustrated MSS. of Terence (C):

Christoph. Henr. Nob. Dom. de Berger, Commentatio de personis, vulgo larvis seu mascheris. Frankfurt u. Leipzig, 1723. This volume contains the pictures in C in all six plays of Terence.

N. Fortiguerra, Terenti Comoediae. Urbini, 1736. This work contains the same pictures as that of Berger, rather more accurately reproduced.

Carolus Coquelines, Publi Terenti Afri Comoediae. Rome, 1767. This book contains essentially what is found in the work of Fortiguerra.

[2] For examples see Wieseler, Denkmäler, XI, 2, 3, 4, 6; Helbig, Campanische Wandgemälde, nos. 1468–1476; Annali d. Inst. 1881, 109 ff.; Mon. d. Inst. XI, tav. 30–32, nos. 2, 5, 10, 14, 16. For further bibliography see Hermann, Lehrbuch der griechischen Antiquitäten, III, 2, 258.

[3] For examples see Wieseler, *l.c.* XI, 1; Annali d. Inst. 1859, tav. d'agg. O and 393 ff. For further references see Hermann, *l.c.*

(4) Statuettes and Roman terra-cottas.[1]

Returning now to the literary evidence, I may say that I have endeavoured to use with special care the testimony of the comedies themselves, regarding them as particularly important because they represent the best period of the Roman theatre.[2] It is unfortunate that the late date of Donatus and Euanthius must always detract from the value of their testimony. Further, we should keep in mind the doubtful character of the text in the passages cited from Pollux and the uncertainty of our right to infer from them the usages of the Roman stage.

Passing to the artistic evidence, I would state that I have examined minutely all the illustra-

---

[1] For examples see Wieseler, *l.c.* XI, 8–11; Bulletino d. Inst. 1870, 58; Archäol. Zeit. 31 (1874), Taf. 12. For additional bibliography see Hermann, *l.c.*

[2] It will appear presently that the costumes indicated by our extant Roman comedies are so simple that it would not have been difficult for the stage-managers, even in the earliest days of the Roman theatre, to be faithful to the indications and descriptions in the plays. The presence of Greek *artifices scaenici* from the very outset of the Roman theatrical productions must be postulated. The term *fabulae palliatae* of itself suggests carefulness in the matter of costumes. In Elizabethan plays, though little emphasis was laid on stage-setting, much stress was laid on costume; see, *e.g.*, H. T. Stephenson, Shakespeare's London (New York, 1906), pp. 320–324.

tions from the manuscripts of Terence which were accessible to me.[1] In many particulars their testimony is sufficiently clear and unanimous to command consideration; yet the danger of relying upon it in disputed points will, I think, become plain as this discussion proceeds. The evidence of the terra-cottas is questionable, because there is no certainty that they actually represent the stock-characters of *fabulae palliatae.* The paintings and reliefs from Campania belong to a section of Italy where Greek influence was strong, if not dominant; they cannot, therefore, be regarded as furnishing, in themselves, any certain evidence for our problem — interesting and valuable though they are when taken in connection with other evidence.

Of the above sources no further description is necessary, except in the case of the illustrated manuscripts of Terence. For the convenience of the reader who may not have access to Bethe's valuable preface to the photographic reproduction of Terenti Codex Ambrosianus H 75 inf. I shall summarize briefly the main facts concerning the miniatures.

There have come to light up to this time twelve MSS. of Terence which are more or less fully

---

[1] For the number and range of these illustrations see Bibliography, pp. 143–144.

illustrated. They range in date from the ninth to the fifteenth century and come, for the most part, from northern France. Of these twelve MSS., three (C, P, F) show illustrations which are evidently rather careful, though indirect,[1] copies of a common original; a fourth (O) reproduces the composition and attitudes of the same original, though the buildings, the clothing, the masks, and the hair have evidently been modernized by the artist. B (Basilicanus Romae in Tabulario Capituli Basilicae Vaticanae 79 H, tenth century) contains only two illustrations, a portrait of Terence on the order of that in C, P, and O, and the *personarum armarium* of the Andria. Q (Berolinensis Meermanianus Latin. 176, fifteenth century) contains a single illustration, a portrait, presumably of Terence. Y (Parisinus Latinus 7900, tenth century) is incomplete and no reproductions of it are at hand. The pictures of the remaining five[2] illustrated

---

[1] It is supposed that there were three copies of the archetype, from one of which were derived the miniatures of C, P, and O, from a second those of F, and from the third those of all the other illustrated MSS.

[2] These MSS. are L (Leidensis Lipsianus 26, tenth century); N (Leidensis Vossianus 38, tenth century); S (Vaticanus 3305, eleventh or twelfth century); T (Terentius Caroli VI Francorum regis nunc Parisiis asservatus in Bibliotheca Arsenalis 25, early fifteenth century); Z (Parisinus Latinus 7903, eleventh century).

MSS. have been so strongly modernized by the artist that they have little value for our purpose.

Our interest centres, therefore, in the four MSS. first mentioned, of which a fuller account may now be given.

C (Vaticanus 3868) contains a portrait of Terence, a *personarum armarium* before each play save the Eunuchus, a representation of the Prologus to each save the Eunuchus, and pictures before all scenes except And. V, 1 and 2. The illustrations are coloured, nine colours being used.[1] The MS. belongs to the ninth century. Since it is doubtless the most valuable of all the illustrated MSS. of Terence, its photographic reproduction, so long promised by Ehrle, is awaited with great interest. Meanwhile, we know it through fragmentary reproductions by Wieseler, Harvard University, Weston, Bethe,[2] and through the un-

---

[1] Ego satis habeo adnotasse coloribus pictorem usum hisce: (1) carnoso qui facies et manus tegat, (2) nigro ad crines imprimis pingendos, (3) cano in vestimentis et pedibus omnium servorum atque in palliis nonnullis et aulaeis, (4) caeruleo in tunicis et pedibus iuvenum senumque, (5) flavo in palliis et ut lignum exprimeret, (6) albo in mulierum tunicis et aulaeis cet., (7) rubro, (8) viridi, (9) fusco. So Bethe, Praefatio 10. It will be seen that the use of colours in the pictures of C does not agree, to any extent, with the statements of Donatus and Pollux.

[2] See Bibliography, pp. 143–144.

reliable reproductions of Berger, Fortiguerra, and Coquelines.[1]

P (Parisinus Latinus 7899) contains the illustrations that are found in C, save that one is lacking at Haut. 954. They are entirely in brown ink, heavily shaded. The artist's work is thus described by Bethe (Praefatio 13): Festinante manu ut videtur et sine accurata illa Vaticani plurimorumque illius aetatis pictorum diligentia et amore sed maiore arte et magis libera P exemplaris antiqui lineas repetivit ita ut picturarum quas imitatus est neque indolem speciemque commutaret, et in ipsis figuris et gestibus, vestibus et ornamentis praestaret fidem omni laude dignam. The MS. is assigned to the ninth century by Chatelain, Traube, and Goldschmidt.[2] It is generally known through the works cited under Bibliography, pp. 143–144.

F (Ambrosianus H 75 inf.) has lost the first leaves up to Eun. III, 2 and the last leaves from Ph. 832. The remainder is fully illustrated to essentially the same extent as C and P, except that the *personarum armarium* of the Hecyra is entirely lacking and that one extra picture is inserted at Haut. 592. The drawings were done in ink; then two colours were laid on — red for faces and hands,

---

[1] See Sources, p. 2, n. 1. [2] See Bethe, Praefatio 13–14.

violet for the hair of all figures and for the clothing and feet of slaves. With these general exceptions the two colours were used indiscriminately for the clothing of old men, young men, and women. Moreover, the garments of the same persons vary in colour in different scenes.[1] It is evident, then, that the testimony of F in this particular is of no value.[2] The MS. is assigned to the early part of the tenth century by Traube and Goldschmidt and to the ninth century by Chatelain.[3] It is, of course, best known to us through the Leyden publication of 1903;[4] the other reliable reproductions of pictures in F may be found under Bibliography, pp. 143–144.

O (Codex Oxoniensis, olim Dunelmensis, nunc Bibliothecae Bodleianae Auct. F 213) was more fully illustrated than C and P, for it contained the pictures before And. V, 1 and 2, and lacked only the masks and the Prologus of the Eunuchus. Several leaves are now lost. The drawings are in ink, shaded. Bethe (Praefatio 16) writes as follows of the artist: Diligenter O singulas archetypi figuras repetivit, sed vestem et portas aedificiaque suae aetatis moribus accommodare stu-

---

[1] See Bethe, Praefatio 20.

[2] Cf. the remark on the value of the colour element in the miniatures of C, p. 6, n. 1.

[3] See Bethe, Praefatio 22.

[4] See Preface, p. vii, n. 1.

duit. Personae quid essent nescivit neque homines personas prae se ferre intellexit. Goldschmidt assigns the MS. to the twelfth century.[1] It is generally known through the works cited under Bibliography, p. 144.

For many years it was the opinion of scholars that the archetype of these four MSS. was exceedingly ancient. Thus Leo[2] placed it after the publication of Varro's Imagines[3] and before the destruction of Pompeii.[4] Bethe,[5] however, concludes that the archetype could not have been earlier than the second century A.D.; he bases his conclusions upon the following considerations:

(1) The fact that at Ph. 348 Crito has a roll and Cratinus a *codex;* our first reliable reference to the use of the *codex* is in Martial 14. 184, 186, 192, *i.e.*, towards the end of the first century A.D.

(2) The architectural peculiarities of the *personarum armaria;* these would even per-

---

[1] See Bethe, Praefatio 16.

[2] Rhein. Mus. 38 (1883), 341 ff.

[3] The first illustrated book at Rome; published about 39 B.C. See Teuffel, § 166. 5.

[4] This *terminus ante quem* was suggested by the marked resemblances between the miniatures and the Pompeian wall scenes.

[5] Praefatio 51–64.

mit a date as late as the third or the fourth century A.D.

(3) The peculiarities of form and setting shown by the portrait of Terence at the beginning of the MSS. These point to a date not earlier than the end of the second century A.D.

This tendency to push the date of the archetype more and more in the direction of our own time is further seen in a recent dissertation[1] by Dr. Otto Engelhardt, whose arguments are briefly these:

(1) The roll remained in use along with the *codex* down to a comparatively late time, as is shown by the mosaics of Christian churches, *e.g.*, St. Apollinare nuovo in Ravenna and, in Rome, San Prassede, St. Agnese, San Lorenzo, and Santa Maria in domnica (pp. 54–55).

(2) The *personarum armaria* show architectural and ornamental forms that run from the second to the fifth century, and some indications point to the later limit (pp. 33–40).

---

[1] Die Illustrationen der Terenzhandschriften. Ein Beitrag zur Geschichte des Buchschmucks, by Otto Engelhardt (Jena, 1905). 97 pp.

(3) The form and ornamentation of the portrait of Terence point to a time not earlier than the fourth century — perhaps as late as the sixth (pp. 25–33).

(4) While there is a large Greek element in the costumes of the miniatures, yet we find many of these same elements persisting until late in the Middle Ages. Cf. the mosaics of San Vitale and St. Apollinare nuovo in Ravenna (fifth and sixth centuries), and the paintings in the Catacombs (pp. 40–57).

(5) The figures are represented as standing on uneven ground, not on a level stage-floor. Some of the pictures depict scenes which, in view of the text, could not have taken place on the stage. In five of the plays the miniatures show the door of a particular house placed now on one side of the stage, now on the other (pp. 58–83).

In view of these reasons Dr. Engelhardt concludes (1) that the pictures are the work of an artist who was a mere illustrator of the text and not the work of a man who was recording an actual stage-presentation of the plays; (2) that the evidence points to the end of the fifth century or the beginning of the sixth; and (3) that, therefore, since the Calliopian recension of Terence was made not earlier than the end of the fifth century,[1] the originals of these pictures were probably made then for the Calliopian recension (pp. 83–92).[2]

In reply it should be said that, although there are some strong resemblances between the costumes of the miniatures and those seen in the paintings of the Catacombs,[3] there are also striking differences, and some of the elements which are most perplexing in the miniatures are not explained at all by those examples of Christian art which Dr. Engelhardt cites. Furthermore, not every one would agree with all of Engelhardt's views on the impossibility of certain scenes.[4] Yet, when we have made allowance for possible over-statement in some particulars, there still remains ample ground for questioning either the value of the archetype or the faithfulness of the descendants to that archetype.

---

[1] While Dziatzko, Schlee, and others assign Calliopius to the fifth century, still others (*e.g.*, Leo) place him as early as the third century. See Fairclough, Andria, Appendix, p. 155.

[2] The illustrated MSS. of Terence all belong to that large class of Terentian MSS. which is connected with the name of Calliopius. The only representative of the other great class is the Bembinus (Vaticanus 3226: A). See Engelhardt, 3.

[3] See Wilpert, Die Malereien der Katakomben Roms (text and plates; Freiburg, 1903).

[4] See, *e.g.*, the discussion of his criticism of the picture of the first scene of the Haut., SENEX, p. 99, n. 3.

As a result of my own study of the pictures, from the standpoint of costume only, I conclude that the artist of the archetype was really attempting to represent *Greek* costumes, such as were worn in *fabulae palliatae,* but that either he did not thoroughly understand the simplest principles of Greek dress or his illustrations have been copied by persons who were decidedly ignorant of those principles. Signs of this ignorance run through the miniatures of all four of the principal illustrated MSS., so far as I have been able to examine them. Therefore, it is probable that part of the fault lies with the original artist — a fact which would tend to discredit the theory of a very early date for the archetype. On the other hand, the four MSS. differ sufficiently among themselves to make it exceedingly difficult, if not impossible, to say how great were the inconsistencies of the original; hence, the impossible costumes found in some of our miniatures may be merely an evidence that ignorant artists were copying something which they did not understand — namely, an *ancient* original.

Many of the difficulties and peculiarities connected with the costumes of the miniatures I shall note as they occur under the individual rôles [1]; for

---

[1] See p. 6, n. 1; p. 8, n. 2; pp. 47, 50, 52, 55, 57, 60, 72, n. 1; 82, 98, 125, etc.

the present I shall summarize briefly the grounds of my general opinion as stated above.

(A) While showing distinct Greek elements and being generally explicable if we suppose an ignorant copyist, certain costumes are *impossible* as truly representing the everyday dress of the Greeks in the time of the New Comedy. It will be sufficient to cite a few out of many examples.

(1) Parallels to Antipho's garment, with its short, flowing sleeves, as seen in C in Ph. 179, 465, 485, and 841, are very familiar to us from P and F; but the artist of C in Ph. 153, 534, and 606 has probably misinterpreted a longitudinal fold in the undergarment as shown in his original and has carried the line of the sleeve almost or quite to the bottom of the tunic-skirt. His picture of Antipho at verse 682 shows a sleeve midway between the two extremes as seen at 179, 465, 485, and 841 on the one side and at 153, 534, and 606 on the other.

(2) In P the overgarment of Simo Senex (And. 796) is impossible as a *pallium* and yet it is clearly intended for a *pallium*, as we shall see if we compare this picture with that of the same person at line 404 and

with the representation of Charinus Adulescens at 625. These latter representations of the *pallium* are not perfectly intelligent, but they are, nevertheless, easily derivable from a perfect *pallium*, and they form a transition from the latter to the anomalous garment of Simo at verse 796.

(3) In F the overgarment of Antipho (Eun. 549) and of Laches Senex (Eun. 971) suggests the same difficulties as that of Simo Senex just described (in P, at And. 796). A confusion of *chlamys* and *pallium* seems to be the explanation of cases like that of Chremes (Eun. 739, in F) and that of Demea (And. 776, in F). This same error is carried over into the costume of a woman in the case of Bacchis (Hec. 726, in F).

(B) Certain costumes are unjustifiable in view of the text; *e.g.*, the costume of Menedemus (Haut. 52–53),[1] that of Pamphilus (And., in P),[2] and that of Chremes, who at Eun. 739 (in F) wears one of those strange overgarments which in some ways resemble a *pallium*, in other ways a *chlamys* (see (A) above), while at the end of the

---

[1] See SENEX, p. 100. [2] See ADULESCENS, p. 48, n. 1.

same scene his *pallium* is mentioned, and in the picture immediately following this reference the artist has drawn a cloak which is clearly a *pallium*.

(C) There are, apparently, capricious changes in costume from scene to scene — changes which probably did not occur on the stage; *e.g.*, in the Eunuchus at verse 540 Antipho wears a *chlamys*, but at 549 his mantle is evidently intended to be a *pallium*, though the probabilities are all against a change of costume here (for further cases of this kind of change see ADULESCENS, p. 47, n. 1). Again, the presence or absence of the ἐγκόμβωμα of Parmeno Servus seems to depend upon the attitude which the artist wishes him to assume (see Eun. 943, 971, 1002, in F).

## CHAPTER II

### TERMINOLOGY

BEFORE we enter upon a detailed discussion of the costumes worn in the individual rôles there are certain terms connected with the general subject of stage-dress in Roman Comedy which we should define.

From several passages in Plautus it is clear that the costumes were supplied by a man known as the Choragus. His function was, therefore, totally different from that of the Greek χορηγός[1]; he was, so far as we can see, merely a professional costumer. When a play was given under governmental supervision, the officials contracted with such a person for the necessary costumes. In the Persa (157–160), where Toxilus and Saturio are discussing the proposed disguise of the latter's daughter, Toxilus says

> Et tu gnatam tuam
> ornatam adduce lepide in peregrinum modum.

Whereupon Saturio inquires Πόθεν *ornamenta?* to which Toxilus answers

---

[1] See, *e.g.*, Smith, Dictionary of Antiquities, *s.v. Choregus*. Cf. also below, p. 19, n. 2.

Abs *chorago* sumito.
Dare debet: praebenda aediles locaverunt.

This frank admission of Toxilus, that he is, after all, merely *acting* in a play, is crude and inartistic, but it has frequent parallels in Plautus,[1] though not in Terence.[2] Perhaps the Sycophanta is making such an admission in Tri. 857–858, when, in speaking of the man who has hired him to disguise himself for purposes of deception, he says,

Ut ille me exornavit, ita sum ornatus: argentum hoc facit.
Ipse ornamenta a *chorago* haec sumpsit suo periculo.

If, on the other hand, the remark is made in good faith by a *real* Sycophanta (*i.e.*, not by a person merely acting a part on the stage), the inference is justifiable that the business of the Choragus was not confined to the theatre.[3] This inference would seem to be borne out by a scene in the Curculio (462–486), where a Choragus is one of the Dramatis Personae and speaks of letting his

---

[1] See Ci. 677, 782 ff.; Men. 880; Mi. 862; Poe. 550; Tri. 990. It is also common in Greek comedy; see, *e.g.*, Aristophanes, Av. 30, 446; Eq. 30; Pax 43; Vesp. 54.

[2] See Euanthius de Fab. III, 8 illud quoque mirabile in eo . . . quod nihil ad populum facit actorem velut extra comoediam loqui, quod vitium Plauti frequentissimum.

[3] Cf. Sonnenschein's Captivi (1880), note on verse 61.

*ornamenta*[1] to Phaedromus, another character in the play (cf. As. 68–72 for a case in which such a disguise may have been undertaken in real life).[2]

The technical term for theatrical costumes seems, from the above cases, to have been *ornamenta.* The word is apparently used in the same sense in several other places, though not in conjunction with the mention of the Choragus. In the Amphitruo, pr. 85, it is used in connection with the actor as such:

> Qui sibi mandasset delegati ut plauderent,
> quive alter quo placeret fecisset minus,
> eius *ornamenta* et corium uti conciderent.

The same use occurs in the Cistellaria (784), where at the end of the play, the Caterva, speaking of Demipho and others who have gone into Melaenis's house to see if Demipho's lost daughter is really there, says

> Ne expectetis, spectatores, dum illi huc ad vos exeant;
> nemo exibit, omnes intus conficient negotium.
> Ubi id erit factum, *ornamenta* ponent: postidea loci,
> qui deliquit vapulabit, qui non deliquit bibet.

---

[1] Ornamenta quae locavi metuo ut possim recipere.
quamquam cum istoc mihi negoti nil est — ipsi Phaedromo
credidi — tamen asservabo. — Cu. 464–466.

[2] On the Choragus see Dziatzko-Hauler, Phormio[3] (1898), p. 34. According to Donatus on Eun. 967 the Choragus

In Cap. 615 *ornamenta* seems to mean the 'conventional stage-costume' of Ajax.[1]

The remaining cases of *ornamenta* in Plautus (when used of *ornàmenta* actually present on the stage) belong mainly[2] to one of two classes; they denote

(1) The costume by which a person is disguised (Poe. 425–426; Ps. 756–757).

(2) Ornaments, in the sense of trinkets, jewelry (Mo. 248,[3] 294).

Terence has the word but once (Haut. 837); it is then used of something not actually on the stage and its meaning is not defined by the context.

The word *choragium* might seem the natural one for denoting the things furnished by the Choragus; yet it occurs only once in Plautus[4] (Cap., pr. 61),

---

served also as stage-manager; of this, however, we have no hint from any other source. See Dziatzko-Hauler, *l.c.*, n. 2.

[1] For the stock-costume of Ulysses, Achilles, and Neoptolemus see Donatus, Exc. de Com. VIII, 4, 5. Cf. Pollux, Onom. IV, 116.

[2] Interesting is St. 172, where *cum ornamentis omnibus* seems to mean 'bag and baggage'; cf. with this Ps. 343, said of a person not present on the stage. The other cases of *ornamenta* used in connection with persons not present on the stage are Men. 804; Mi. 106, 981, 1127, 1147, 1302; Tru. 318.

[3] Cf. Lorenz's note.

[4] Neither *choragus* nor *choragium* is found in Terence.

where the Prologus, assuring the spectators that the mention of war does not imply that a tragedy is to be forced upon them though they like comedy so much better, says

> Nam hoc paene iniquomst, comico *choragio*
> conari desubito agere nos tragoediam.

One feels that *choragium* here includes not only the costumes, but all the necessary properties and stage-apparatus for the production of a play; such an interpretation, further, is in line with Festus's definition of *choragium* as *instrumentum scaenarum.*[1] In the time of the Empire we hear of a special building where all the imperial stage-apparatus was kept and the person in charge of this branch of the Emperor's service was styled *procurator summi choragi.* This procurator was himself a freedman of the imperial household, and there was associated with him a host of minor officials, partly freedmen, partly slaves, called *adiutores, tabularii, dispensatores, contra scriptores,* and *medici rationis summi choragi.* A subdivision of this *ratio summi choragi* seems to have been known as the *ratio ornamentorum,* whose chief care was the costumes of actors.[2]

---

[1] Cf. Vitruvius 5. 91 post scenam porticus sunt constituendae uti . . . choragia laxamentum habeant ad comparandum.

[2] For further information on this period see Hirschfeld, Die

*Ornamenta*, then, is always the word used of costume in connection with the mention of the Choragus, but *ornatus* often comes close to *ornamenta* in the general sense of costume. In only one passage does it seem to me at all to justify the interpretation 'stage-attire' — viz. in the first verse of the second prologue of the Hecyra —

Orator ad vos venio *ornatu prologi* —

and this proves little because Terence's Prologus is so essentially a *stage*-character; he does not exist in real life.

The substantive *ornatus* [1] seems generally to be used by Plautus in the sense of 'garb,' 'attire.' [2] In some cases the idea of 'disguise' may be close at hand, notably in Poe. 801 (cf. Mi. 1286).

Occasionally the substantive *ornatus* seems to refer to some article carried, or in use, by the person described, as, possibly, to a bucket carried by Ampelisca (Ru. 431) [3] or to a pick-axe used by Callicles Senex in digging for the buried treasure

---

kaiserlichen Verwaltungsbeamten bis auf Diocletian,[2] 293-297.

[1] Ornatus dicitur et bonis artibus instructus et honores adeptus, appellatur quoque ornatus cultus ipse quo quis ornatus. . . . So Festus, p. 205 (Thewrewk de Ponor).

[2] See Am., pr. 116, 1007; Mer. 910-912 ('attire,' 'equipment'); Mi. 899, 1177, 1282, 1286; Per. 463; Poe. 283; Ps. 935; Ru. 293; Tri. 840 b, 852.

[3] Cf. Ru. 432.

(Tri. 1099). Sometimes the notion of properties that form no part of costume is perhaps the only one (Ba. 110, 125; Cu. 2). In Tru. 475 both costume and other properties seem to be included in *ornatus*. All these meanings lie very near the essential notion of the verb *ornare*, 'to equip' (Mo. 291; Poe. 306, 307).[1] Not far to seek is the meaning of the word in Cas. 932, 974, Ru. 187, in which cases 'plight' is a fair translation.

In Ep. 577 *ornatus*[2] is used with *vestitus*, perhaps pleonastically, perhaps as a more inclusive word.

Besides the case cited above (Hec., pr. II, 1) Terence shows three[3] examples of the substantive *ornatus*. In And. 365 it apparently does not refer to costume at all, but to the general holiday appearance of a house prepared for a wedding. In Eun. 237 Gnatho tells about meeting a friend whose life had been less prosperous than his own; the man, who was dirty and ragged, to Gnatho's question, *quid istuc ornatist?* said

---

[1] Cf. Men. 146 and 709; in the former case Menaechmus I has put on his wife's *palla*, in 709 Menaechmus II is probably carrying the same *palla*.

[2] The few cases of the substantive *ornatus* used by Plautus of persons not present on the stage at the time suggest no peculiar meanings for the word.

[3] Of course I do not include in this number Eun., Per. 9.

quoniam miser quod habui perdidi, em
quo redactus sum. omnes me noti atque amici deserunt.

In Eun. 546 the reference is to the costume of Chaerea gotten up as the Eunuchus.

The participle *ornatus* is common in the sense of 'dressed,' 'attired,' 'adorned.'[1] The idea of 'plight' referred to above (p. 23), in connection with the substantive *ornatus*, is in the participle in Ru. 187, 488, while the use of the substantive with reference to an article carried (Ru. 431; Tri. 1099) is paralleled by the use of the participle in Ru. 908, where the allusion is to the *vidulus* which Gripus has fished up. In Ep. 194 the sentence is probably pleonastic and Epidicus *se ornat* ('equips,' 'prepares himself,' for running) by gathering up his *pallium* on his shoulder (see SERVUS, pp. 106–108).

In the cases in which the verb *ornare* is used by Plautus in connection with scenes not present to the spectator the purpose of the 'equipment' often causes the idea of 'disguise' to lie near at hand (Mi. 791, 1195). The idea of giving a house a festive appearance for a wedding is in the verb in Cas. 546, as it was in the substantive *ornatus* in And. 365 (p. 23). The original idea of 'equipping'

---

[1] See Am., pr. 119; Cap. 997; Cas. 540; Mi. 872, 897; Mo. 249; Per. 158; Ru. 573; etc.

comes to the fore in Poe. 214–215, perhaps wholly through the inclusion of a ship in the subject. In Cap. 447 *ornatus* means 'attended' by a person whose presence is desired. In Ru. 730 the force is 'with such a dressing (beating) that you won't know yourself.' In Cas. 578 and Ps. 676 it is used of things 'arranged,' 'made ready.'

In Terence we find *ornatus* used in And. 176 in the same sense as in Ru. 730. In Haut. 288 it is merely 'dressed,' 'adorned.' In Eun. 213 the verb signifies to 'adorn,' in a transferred sense (cf. Ph. 853). In Eun. 377 it suggests 'disguise.'

The verb *exornare* is generally stronger than *ornare*[1] and means to 'deck out,' 'adorn elaborately' (cf., *e.g.*, Mo. 290, 293; St. 744), to 'get up' (cf., *e.g.*, Per. 462; Tri. 767), to 'fit out' (cf., *e.g.*, Ps. 751, 757), etc. Often the idea of 'disguise' is not far to seek (cf., *e.g.*, Cas. 769; Mi. 1184; Per. 335). Interesting in connection with the use of *ornare* in And. 365 and Cas. 546 (see p. 24) is that of *exornare* in Au. 784, where a wedding is being 'prepared for.'

The two cases of the verb *exornare* in Terence

---

[1] Cases like As. 670–671; Poe. 283–285; Tri. 857 are only apparent exceptions to this statement, for the force of the compound verb is felt in the simple verb that follows (cf. also Euripides, Alc. 400; Medea 1252, with Earle's note). In Poe. 213–214, however, *exornare* is perhaps not especially strong.

both contain the participle *exornatus;* of these, one (Eun. 683) shows the meaning 'dressed,' 'adorned,' the other (Haut. 950) is interesting as being parallel with *ornatus* of Ru. 730.

Unique in Plautus and Terence is the diminutive *exornatula* shown in Ci. 306.

*Vestimentum, vestis,* and *vestitus* are all used by Plautus and Terence. Festus says, *Vestis* generaliter dicitur, ut stragula, forensis, muliebris: *vestimentum* pars aliqua, ut pallium, tunica, penula.

The latter definition applies in Men. 167 and 659, where the *vestimentum muliebre* is the *palla* of the wife of Menaechmus I; but in most other cases in Plautus *vestimentum* is more general in force, equalling 'garments' (Ru. 528, 573) or, even more vaguely, 'clothing' (Per. 669). This seems also to be true of the word when used of something not actually on the stage at the time; see, *e.g.*, As. 92; Ba. 482; Cu. 415; Ep. 224; Cas. 258; Ep. 216; Ru. 383, 574; Tru. 137.

*Vestimentum* occurs but once in Terence, in Haut. 141, where it appears in a set phrase, *vas et vestimentum,* furnishing no evidence of the exact meaning.

The force of *vestis,* as defined by Festus (see above), is fairly well borne out by Plautine usage, but St. 350 presents an exception (so, too, perhaps, Ep. 229 ff.). Common in both Plautus and Terence is the collocation *aurum et* (*atque*) *vestem*.[1] In other respects, too, Terence's use of *vestis* is frequent and regular.

Both Plautus and Terence use *vestitus* as a general word for clothing. Interesting is the combination *petasum ac vestitum* (Am. 443), as if *vestitus* were limited to garments. The verb *vestire* commonly occurs in the passive and means 'clothed.'[2] Worthy of note in connection with the frequent collocation *aurum et* (*atque*) *vestem* mentioned above is *auratam et vestitam* (Men. 801) and *vestita, aurata, ornata* (Ep. 222).

I do not detect any stage-colouring in the use of *vestimentum, vestis, vestitus,* or *vestire.*

*Habitus*, as 'clothing,' 'dress,' is not much used before the Augustan period and, except for Poe. 238 and 288, is found in the texts under discussion only in Arg. II, 4 of the Amphitruo and in Per. 8 of the Hautontimorumenos.

---

[1] Cu. 348, 489; Ci. 487; Mi. 1099. Cf. *aurum* (*atque*) *ornamenta*, Mi. 981, 1127, 1147.

[2] Exceptional are St. 376 ('to furnish clothing for') and Haut. 130 ('to make garments for').

## CHAPTER III

### PROLOGUS

THE question of the costume worn by the Prologus in Roman Comedy is complicated by the fact that a gradual development took place in his nature and function.

Examining the twenty available plays of Plautus, we find that the opening lines of the Bacchides are lost, and that the opening scene of four other plays (Cu., Ep., Per., St.) is a dialogue that serves to set forth the situation, but that in each of the remaining fifteen plays there appears what is technically known as a prologue. Of these fifteen prologues, eight (Am., Mer., Mi., Mo., Au., Ru., Tri., Ci.) are of a Greek type, consisting of a monologue,[1] spoken in the case of the first four by a character in the play, in the case of the last four by a god or allegorical character. The speakers of the former class obviously require no separate treatment as Prologi; for the discussion of the latter class see pp. 39 ff. The remaining seven

[1] The dialogue element in the prologue of Tri. (see p. 40) is hardly sufficient to place that prologue in a separate class.

plays — or, more accurately, six, for we cannot speak with certainty of the scanty remains of the prologue to the Pseudolus — open with the discourse of a person known as the Prologus, a character who has no rôle in the play proper, but whose function is merely to introduce the play, generally by relating the plot. This Prologus, whom Fabia [1] describes as a personification of the prologue itself, the ancients associated with the Roman, as opposed to the Greek, stage.[2]

The prologues of Terence represent a still greater detachment from the plays, for no one of them concerns itself with narrating the plot; they are all defences of the poet against the accusations of his enemies.[3]

---

[1] Les Prologues de Térence, 84.

[2] Euanthius de Fabula III,2 tum etiam Graeci prologos non habent more nostrorum, quos Latini habent. Deinde θεοὺς ἀπὸ μηχανῆς, id est deos argumentis narrandis machinatos, ceteri Latini ad instar Graecorum habent, Terentius non habet.

[3] Cf. And., pr. 1 ff. This element of literary polemic in his prologues had long been regarded as an innovation of Terence, but traces of it have been found in a fragmentary Greek prologue, discovered in a collection of papyri (Pap. Graec. 53) at Strassburg and published in 1899. It is, however, worthy of notice that, though the poet under the guise of a god seems in part of the Strassburg prologue to be justifying himself and his new technique against his rivals, he *goes on to relate the argumentum.* For a discussion of the subject see Reitzenstein, Hermes 35 (1900), 622; Kroll, Bursian's Jahresber. 124 (1905, Supp.-Band), 22.

### (A) *Roman Type*

The sole *literary* evidence for a special Prologus-costume is in the first line of the second prologue to Terence's Hecyra,

> Orator ad vos venio *ornatu prologi.*

Wagner's assumption[1] that Poe., pr. 127

> Valete, adeste: ibo, *alius fieri* nunc volo

confirms the theory of such a costume is not inevitable; indeed, even the contrary inference is possible, if one reads verse 123

> Ego ibo, *ornabor*: vos aequo animo noscite

with unprejudiced mind.[2]

Since, then, the ancients give no information concerning the costume of the Prologus, it becomes necessary for those who maintain its existence to consider what costume would have been suitable in view of the nature and function of the Prologus. The general argument of scholars proceeds along the following lines.

First, from Haut., pr. 1–2,

> Nequoi sit vostrum mirum, quor partes seni
> poeta dederit, quae sunt adulescentium,

[1] See Wagner's Terentii Comoediae, 344; also his Studien zu Terentius, Jahrbücher für Class. Phil. 11 (1865), 282 ff.

[2] Lindsay would refuse to accept this evidence, for he says

we see that the rôle belonged to *adulescentes*. Next, from Cap. 61–62, Cas. 22, Ph. 30–33, Ad. 3, we may assume, and from Poe. 123,[1] 126, Haut. 5, 39 ff., we know, that the Prologus was one of the actors comprising the theatrical troupe. Finally, the Prologus of the Poenulus, at least, also played one of the rôles of the play proper (126).

Very natural, therefore, is the common conclusion that this rôle of Prologus was assigned to the young, inexperienced members of the *grex*, because it made no demand on histrionic powers; what it did require was, first and foremost, good, sound lungs, in order that the speaker might silence and bring to order a noisy Roman audience.[2]

In an interesting chapter (II) of his Les Prologues de Térence Fabia attempts to determine the probable costume of the Terentian Prologus. We may summarize his argument as follows: The Prologus, being an outgrowth of a Dramatis Persona in Greek comedy, would, according to the practice of all other characters in *fabulae palliatae*, wear Greek costume. Furthermore, being an

---

"121–123 retractatori tribuo, alterum exitum (124–128) ipsi Plauto." [1] See p. 30, n. 2.

[2] See, *e.g.*, the Poe. prologue and both prologues of the Hecyra.

*adulescens*, he would wear the costume of *adulescentes;* but, since it might easily happen that a bona fide Adulescens would come on the stage in the opening scene of the play proper,[1] this *adulescens*-Prologus needed some peculiar insignia by which the audience might immediately recognize him as Prologus. Now, since he was a sort of ambassador of the poet, a suppliant beseeching the favour of the audience for the play and for the poet, he might well have carried the insignia

---

[1] As a matter of fact, in only one play of Terence, the Eun., is an Adulescens on the stage in the opening scene of the play, and there, since he is not alone but is accompanied by Parmeno Servus, there would be no danger of his being confused with a Prologus. In the seven Plautine plays with a 'Roman' Prologus the opening scenes show on the stage the following characters:

As. — Servus and Senex.
Cap. — Parasitus.
Cas. — Two Servi.
Men. — Parasitus.
Poe. — Adulescens and Servus.
Ps. — Adulescens and Servus.
Tru. — Adulescens.

The Parasitus would probably be in no danger of being confused with an adulescens-Prologus (see Stock-rôles, PARASITUS), the Senex and Servus would certainly be recognizable, the Adulescens of Scene 1 in Poe. and Ps. is not alone, so that the Truculentus is our only extant play with a 'Roman' Prologus in which an Adulescens comes on the stage alone at the beginning of the first scene. Of all the other plays of Plautus only two show an Adulescens in Scene 1: in the Curculio he is accompanied by a Servus; in the Mercator Charinus Adulescens relates the *argumentum* in a long monologue.

of suppliants and ambassadors — *i.e.*, branches wound with fillets.[1]

It will be simplest to examine the last part of this theory first — the conjecture regarding the peculiar insignia of the Prologus. Its support was, apart from its mere possibility, the evidence of three Terentian miniatures, — those of the Prologus Ad. (P) and of the Prologi Ad. and Ph. (C).[2] In P, says Fabia, the Prologus Ad. carries a very long branch resembling the palm; in C his branch, which is much shorter and broader, it is impossible to identify.[3] The Prologus Ph. in C bears a branch whose narrow leaves suggest to Fabia the olive. In all three cases the branch is in the left hand, the right hand being left free for gesticulation.

I have had access to six miniatures of Prologi not known to Fabia — the four shown in F[4] and two (And. and Ph.) from O. In these six only one Prologus (Ad., F) carries a branch. To put it

---

[1] For the *supplex* cf. Liv. 24. 30. 14; 29. 16. 6; Tac. Hist. 1. 66; for the *legatus* see Verg. Aen. 7. 154, 237; 8. 116; 9. 231.

[2] Codices F and (apparently) O were not known to Fabia. P he knew at first hand.

[3] This is not entirely due to the fact that Fabia knew C not directly but only through the untrustworthy reproductions of Berger and Coquelines (p. 2, n. 1), for the branch of the Ph. Prologus (C) in the Harvard reproductions (see Weston in Bibliography) is almost equally unrecognizable.

[4] Prologi And. and Eun. are lacking in F.

briefly, then, in C, P, and F, our three [1] best illustrated MSS., only four cases are found in which the Prologus carries a branch; of these, again, three represent the Prologus of a single play — the Adelphoe. Furthermore, in not a single one of the four cases does the branch show any trace of fillets.

It is, therefore, clear that Fabia's conjecture, plausible and attractive as it seems, is supported by very slight evidence. One may, of course, say with him that in the archetype all Prologi carried branches, but that in the descendants, C, P, and F, only four miniatures of Prologi have been completed on the model furnished by the archetype. Such a supposition is, to be sure, possible, but it hardly commends itself to one's judgment as probable.

In view of the comparatively small number (4) of cases of Prologi bearing branches, it seems reasonable to regard them as exceptions rather than as the norm, and, since three of the four represent the Prologus of a single play (Ad., C, P, and F [2]), one is tempted, in the case of that play at least, to seek the explanation of the branch in the peculiar circumstances of the production

[1] It is impossible to draw conclusions about the Prologi in O on the evidence of two miniatures.

[2] Prologus Ad. (O) is not at hand.

of the play. Indeed, Mme. Dacier, who believed the branch in Ad. (C) to be of cypress, long ago suggested [1] the special fitness of such an emblem, since the play was acted for the first time at the funeral games of Aemilius Paulus. Though the branch is probably not of cypress, but of palm, the latter would be even more appropriate at games held in honour of a great conqueror and conspicuous citizen.

It remains to account for the branch carried by the Prologus of the Phormio in C. This alone of all Terence's plays was produced for the first time at the Ludi Romani. Now, the Ludi Romani were instituted for the celebration of triumphs — Ludi Maximi they were called and Ludi Maximi they were in fact. In view of this, what is more natural than that the Prologus of a play to be given for the first time at this festival should bear a branch of palm or of olive? [2] In accepting such an explanation we must admit the failure of the artist to add the original branch of the archetype in P, F, and O; but that objection applies with equal force to almost all possible theories.

---

[1] Cf. Wieseler, Denkmäler, 71; also Fabia, 164, and the picture of Prologus Ad. (F).

[2] Weston, Harvard Studies, 14. 53, thinks the branch may be of palm; Fabia, 164, holds that it is of olive.

Having thus rejected the supposition that the Prologus, merely as Prologus, carried a fillet-wound branch, we must next examine Fabia's main contention that the *ornatus Prologi* of the second prologue of the Hecyra was, at bottom, the *ornatus Adulescentis* (in the technical sense of ADULESCENS, as a Stock-rôle; see pp. 42–52). Immediately, the following facts concerning the miniatures of Prologi cast discredit upon such a contention:

(1) In C, P, and F the Prologus of the Ph. is the only *adulescens*[1]-Prologus, and in O even this Prologus is not clearly young.
(2) In C, P, and F the Prologi of Haut., Ad., and Hec. are *Senes*.[1]
(3) In C and P the Prologus of the And. is a *Servus*[1] (in F he is lacking).
(4) In C the Prologus of the Eun. seems to be a *Servus* (in P and F he is lacking).
(5) In O the character of the only Prologi available is hard to identify; that the Prologus Ph. is an *Adulescens* (as in C, P, and F) and that the Prologus And. is a *Servus* (as in C and P) is by no means sure.

---

[1] For the marks by which this character is recognizable see under Stock-rôles, pp. 42–52, 92–100, 100–108.

One may say, as does Fabia, that the artist of the archetype represented all Prologi as *Adulescentes*, save the Prologus of the Haut.[1] and the second Prologus of the Hec.,[1] to whom he correctly gave the face of a *Senex* and then ignorantly gave the *costume* of a Senex, and that later scribes, finding both Adulescentes and Senes serving as Prologi, concluded that any male character might fill the rôle and so represented the Prologus now as Adulescens, now as Senex, now as Servus. Again, I admit that such a thing *may* have happened; but the miniatures of the other characters are by no means so capriciously done.

I am inclined to believe that Fabia has interpreted too narrowly the word *adulescentium* of Haut., pr. 2. and to hold that Ambivius Turpio did not use the term in its technical, stage sense, but rather that he used it loosely of any man young in years, whether bond or free.[2] Thus it is used by Plautus in addressing a slave (Ci. 597, 731; Ep. 1; Men. 1021, 1025, 1065; Per. 597; Ru. 416, 563), a cook (Men. 285), a parasite (Men. 498, 506), a fisherman (Ru. 1303), a soldier (Ep.

---

[1] These prologues were spoken by Ambivius Turpio, a Senex (Haut., pr. 1, 43; Hec., pr. II, 2), under whose auspices all of Terence's plays, as originally brought out in the lifetime of the poet, were produced.

[2] The Adulescens as a Stock-rôle is the young gentleman in the etymological sense.

440, 444, 459; Poe. 1307), a *trapezita* (Cu. 399), etc. Terence uses it in addressing a parasite (Ph. 378); in Hec. 661 a young woman is referred to as *adolescens mulier* (cf. And. 488). Furthermore, that absolute identity and uniformity of make-up for the Roman Prologus may easily have been a matter of indifference is rendered probable by the fact that the function of the Prologus is always speedily made known by his lines without the aid of peculiar costume and insignia. Lastly, the marked lack of uniformity exhibited by his Greek prototype, if it has any weight in the matter, argues for variety rather than for uniformity in the case of the Roman Prologus.

On such a supposition the varying representations in C, P, and F are explicable, for the only troublesome miniature, that of the *senex*-Prologus of the Adelphoe, might easily have resulted from a misunderstanding on the part of the original artist, since this play was presented at the same time with the third presentation of the Hecyra, whose Prologus was Ambivius Turpio Senex. It is hardly conceivable that there should have been so great a variation as the miniatures show from a norm that was at all well supported by tradition.

Thus, finally, we return to the interpretation of the line from which we started (Hec., pr. II, 1):

Orator ad vos venio ornatu prologi.

Here Ambivius Turpio was probably made up as a young man,[1] but in the other case where he spoke a prologue (Haut.), he was dressed as a Senex, since there he had to come on in the first scene of the play as a Senex.[2]

## (B) *Greek Type*

Of this type we need discuss only that class in which gods[3] or allegorical characters serve as Prologi (cf. p. 28).

(1) The prologue of the Amphitruo is spoken by Mercurius, who is at the same time a Dramatis Persona. Since he is to counterfeit Sosia, he appears *cum servili schema* (117). For discussion see Unusual Rôles, Dɪ, pp. 119–120.

(2) The prologue of the Aulularia is spoken by

---

[1] For the rôle which he probably played in the Hecyra cf. Donatus, Hec., Praef. 4: atque in hac primae partes sunt Lachetis, secundae Pamphili, tertiae Phidippi, quartae Parmenonis et deinceps aliarum personarum, quae his adiunctae sunt. See also Haut., pr. 35–45. One may not agree with Donatus concerning the relative importance of the rôles of Laches and Pamphilus; but whichever part Ambivius Turpio played, he did not appear in Act I.

[2] Cf. Bentley, Haut., pr. 1–3; Flickinger, Class. Phil. 2. 2. 160 ff.

[3] That it was not unusual for gods to come on the stage in *tragedy* is seen in Am., pr. 41–42, 88–90.

Lar Familiaris. His costume is not sufficiently distinctive to insure his recognition by the audience, for he says (Au. 1–3):

> Ne quis miretur qui sim, paucis eloquar.
> Ego Lar sum familiaris ex hac familia
> unde exeuntem me aspexistis.

However, Fabia's conjecture that the Lar wore garlands is reasonable (Au. 25).[1]

(3) The passage which is in effect the prologue of the Cistellaria is introduced after two scenes of the play have been presented. It is spoken by Auxilium Deus, who seems to fear, as did Lar Familiaris in the Aulularia, that he may not be recognized by the spectators (Ci. 149–155). He gives no clue to his make-up.

(4) The prologue of the Rudens is appropriately spoken by Arcturus. Probably the god wore a star[2] on his brow (Ru., pr. 3–4).

(5) The Trinummus is the only extant Roman Comedy in which we find a dialogue between allegorical characters. The speakers, Luxuria and

---

[1] For confirmation of this conjecture see Helbig, Campanische Wandgemälde, p. 19, 60 b, and Mau-Kelsey, Pompeii, p. 270. The Lares here represented are crowned, carry drinking-horns and *situlae,* wear high boots, high-girt tunics, and scarf-like mantles wound more or less closely about the shoulders and body.

[2] Cf. the star on the helmets of Castor and Pollux as shown on Roman coins.

Inopia, give us no clue concerning their costume, but we may easily believe that it suited their characters, especially since the allegory and the dialogue element — slight though it is — render this an unusually dramatic prologue.

## CHAPTER IV

### STOCK-RÔLES

#### ADULESCENS

THE rôle of Adulescens is very common, occurring at least once in every play of Plautus, save the Amphitruo, Casina, Persa, and Stichus, and from one to four times in each of Terence's plays. In spite of this fact, however, there is very little evidence in the comedies themselves about the costume of the Adulescens. From the following passages the *pallium* would seem to be the usual outer garment:

(1) In the Mercator (911 ff.) Charinus Adulescens, about to give up the expedition in search of his love, wishes to lay aside the *chlamys* of the soldier [1] (see Stock-rôles, MILES) and calls for his *pallium*, as if it were his usual garment.

(2) In Tri. 624 Lysiteles grasps Lesbonicus Adulescens by his *pallium*.

(3) In Eun. 769 Thais calls to Chremes Adu-

---

[1] For the quasi-military nature of the expedition see Charinus's words, Mer. 851–854. See also below, pp. 79–80.

lescens, who is just leaving the stage, *Attolle pallium.*

The plays give us no evidence about the tunic [1] of the Adulescens.

Concerning the colour of his garments we read in Donatus, De Com. VIII, 6: comicis senibus candidus vestitus inducitur, quod is antiquissimus fuisse memoratur, adulescentibus discolor [2] attribuitur. Pollux,[3] writing of the costumes in comedy, says (Onom. IV, 119): φοινικὶς ἢ μελαμπόρφυρον ἱμάτιον φόρημα νεωτέρων . . . καὶ πορφυρᾷ [4] ἐσθῆτι ἐχρῶντο οἱ νεανίσκοι. That the clothing might be very fine is inferred from such passages as Ad. 62–63,[5] where Demea Senex chides his brother Micio for indulging Aeschinus in extravagant ways:

---

[1] Professor Fowler's note on Men. 910, from which one might infer that Menaechmus I did not wear a *long*-sleeved tunic, receives no justification from the text.

[2] "Ce que signifie que les différentes pièces du vêtement ne sont pas de même couleur. . . . Il ne faudrait pas entendre par 'discolor vestitus' un vêtement begarré. Cette idée est exprimée plus loin à propos du leno par ces mots: Leno pallio varii coloris utitur." So Fabia, Les Prologues de Térence, 159; cf. below, p. 66.

[3] My citations are from Dindorf's edition of the Onomasticon of Pollux.

[4] For Wieseler's attempt to reconcile these statements of Donatus and Pollux see Denkmäler, 80 a.

[5] Cf. Morris's note on Lysiteles Adulescens, Tri. 223.

quor tu his rebus sumptum suggeris,
vestitu nimio indulges?

In the Mostellaria (384), Callidamates, drunken and sleepy, is partially aroused from the couch where he is reclining by news of the arrival of Philolaches's father, and says:

ain tu, pater?
cedo *soleas* mi, ut arma capiam. iam pol ego occidam patrem.

Similarly, in the Truculentus (363–367), Diniarchus, angrily starting to withdraw from an imaginary banquet with Phronesium Meretrix, cries out:

cedo *soleas* mihi.
properate, auferte mensam.

Presently, when he has been reconciled to her, he says:

iam rediit animus. deme *soleas*, cedo bibam.

From Diomedes[1] we get information about the hair of the Dramatis Personae: antea itaque galearibus, non personis utebantur, ut qualitas coloris indicium faceret aetatis, cum essent aut albi aut nigri aut rufi. Young men are therefore generally supposed to have worn dark or black wigs. Interesting, then, is the case of Philo-

[1] Keil, Gram. Lat. 1. 489.

crates Captivus, who is, in his absence, described by his countryman Aristophontes as follows (Cap. 647–648):

macilento ore, naso acuto, corpore albo, oculis nigris, *subrufus aliquantum, crispus, cincinnatus.*

Two matters here deserve notice, the colour of the hair and its arrangement. It may be that Philocrates, who had been disguised as a slave in the first part of the play, was therefore represented with red[1] hair, so that the exigencies of the plot compelled Aristophontes to describe him thus, *adulescens* though Philocrates was to his countryman. If we take this view, we shall be obliged to credit Plautus with having taken great care on a somewhat minute point. Yet, after all, the red hair scarcely needs explanation in view of the passage just cited from Diomedes. It is to be noted that Diomedes does not specifically assign black hair to the Adulescens and red to the Servus. We shall see in the discussion of the Servus (pp. 102–103) that the evidence for red hair as a standing characteristic of slaves is somewhat limited. Interesting in this connection is the description of Plesidippus (Ru. 313, *rubicundum*).

Just as *crispus* and *cincinnatus* were used of

[1] See SERVUS, pp. 102–103.

Philocrates in the lines quoted above, so Dinarchus in the Truculentus is *cincinnatus* (610–611), but in the latter passage the whole description implies reproach.[1]

In Ep. 646 Stratippocles probably has a *crumina;* in Men. 272, 384–386 Menaechmus II, as a traveller,[2] has a *marsuppium.*

The elaborate description of Pleusicles, disguised as a sailor (Mi. 1177–1184, 1282, 1286, 1306–1309, 1312, 1430: see p. 127), has, of course, no bearing on his rôle as Adulescens.

Pollux, beginning his chapter Περὶ ὑποδημάτων καὶ ἐσθήτων τραγικῶν καὶ κωμικῶν καὶ λοιπῆς σκευῆς, writes as follows (Onom. IV, 115): καὶ τὰ ὑποδήματα, κόθορνοι μὲν τὰ τραγικὰ καὶ ἐμβάδες. ἐμβάται δὲ, τὰ κωμικά. Now ἐμβάδες and ἐμβάται (or ἔμβατα) were contrasted by the Greeks as *cothurni* and *socci* were contrasted by the Romans (Hor. A. P. 80, 90; Ov. Rem. Am. 976; Mart. 8. 3. 13; etc., etc.).

---

[1] *Cincinnatus* commonly means 'artificially curled.' The familiarity of the cognomen Cincinnatus would, however, probably operate to prevent the term from inevitably conveying a reproach.

[2] The traveller is generally represented in *chlamys* and *petasus.* There is no reason, however, why he may not often have worn the *pallium;* indeed, Plautus shows cases of the *pallium* worn on the journey (Labrax Leno, Ru. 549–550) and as the traveller comes home from the harbour (Sosia Servus, Am. 294). For a full discussion of the costume of travellers as seen in Plautus and Terence see Knapp, Class. Phil. 2. 295–300.

The *soccus* was regarded as belonging with the *pallium* and was, therefore, suitable in *fabulae palliatae* (for further discussion see Wieseler, Denkmäler, 77 a).

TESTIMONY OF THE MINIATURES

I have examined about one hundred and forty representations of the Adulescens in the illustrated MSS. of Terence. Of these, approximately three-sevenths show the *pallium;* the rest show a *chlamys*-like mantle, which is fastened regularly on the right shoulder with a clasp. Indeed, these two types of outer garment seem to be used quite indifferently, a given character being represented now with the *pallium*, now with the *chlamys*-like mantle, within the limits of a few lines. Moreover, two Adulescentes may wear, one the *pallium*, the other the *chlamys*, and in the following scene the costumes may be reversed, while in a third scene both may wear one and the same kind of garment.[1] For the bearing of such cases on the value of the miniatures see p. 16. Though Plautus does not speak of the *chlamys* in connection with an Adulescens *as such*, and though the word is not found in

---

[1] See, *e.g.*, Clinia and Clitipho, Haut., F. At 230, Clinia wears the *pallium* and Clitipho the *chlamys*-like mantle; at 242, Clinia has the *chlamys* and Clitipho the *pallium*, while in the next scene (381) both wear the *chlamys*.

Terence, the use of this garment for the Athenian ἔφηβος is correct.[1] The difficulty lies in its apparently erratic and certainly inconsistent use in the miniatures.[2]

The evidence of the miniatures of Adulescentes is overwhelmingly on the side of a rather close, long-sleeved undergarment.[3] In the examples of O available only this long sleeve is visible, but in C, P, and F there usually appears, over this long, close sleeve, a short, flowing sleeve reaching about to the elbow. The natural interpretation is that

---

[1] Τὸ δὲ τῶν ἐφήβων φόρημα, πέτασος καὶ χλαμύς, says Pollux, Onom. X, 164. Chaerea Adulescens in the Eunuchus (824) was an ἔφηβος. Pamphilus (And. 51) is referred to as one who *excessit ex ephebis;* the only miniatures of him at my disposal are from P, where he generally wears a *pallium*, though in three cases (301, 338, 412) his mantle is *chlamys*-like. Wieseler is mistaken in identifying the figure of the young man in Tafel X, n. 4, with Pamphilus: the picture is from Eun. 207 and the youth is Phaedria. On the ἔφηβος in Plautus and Terence see also Knapp, Class. Phil. 2. 14.

[2] The only examples of Adulescentes which are accessible to me from O show the *chlamys*-like mantle.

[3] The only exceptions are:

(*a*) Chremes (Eun. 910, F), who stands between two women, an *ancilla* and a *nutrix*, whose garments, like those of Chremes, show only the short, flowing sleeve.

(*b*) Chaerea (Eun. 1031, F), with only the short, flowing sleeve, though in the next picture (1049) he has both kinds.

The long sleeves of Antipho (Ad. 540, F) and of Phaedria (Ph. 485, O), while not very plainly indicated, are nevertheless there, I believe.

the long sleeves belong with an inner tunic and the short, flowing sleeves with an outer tunic, which ordinarily is long enough to conceal the skirt of the inner garment. Such an interpretation is supported by a small number of miniatures, like those of Clinia at Haut. 679 (F) and of Aeschinus at Ad. 261 (F); in these cases the outer tunic is girt up high enough to show the skirt of the inner.[1]

That the χιτὼν χειριδωτός[2] was regarded by the

[1] It may be that the short oversleeve is the result of a misinterpretation of the *pallium* when worn over the right arm. Yet the colouring of the short sleeve, in the few coloured miniatures at my disposal, is like that of the tunic, not like that of the *pallium*.

[2] See Smith, Dictionary of Greek and Roman Antiquities,[3] 2. 903 ff., where we read of long sleeves "In art such sleeves form part of the typical Asiatic costume on vase-paintings and other monuments. Yet even in the monuments there are figures like the handmaid on the gravestone of Thrasiklea, under STELE, with quite tight sleeves. They also are sometimes seen on old men; and, to judge by the inscriptions in which χειριδωτὸς χιτωνίσκος is mentioned, were in common use among women. In later times a sleeved shirt formed part of the traditional costume of the comic actor." See also Smith, 1. 814, *s.v. Exomis.* Hermann, however, says (Lehrbuch, 231) the long-sleeved χιτών belonged to tragedy. Baumeister, 2. 825 A, *s.v. Lustspiel*, writes thus: "Die Gewandung der neuen Komödie entspricht im allgemeinen derjenigen des gewöhnlichen Lebens. Die freien Männer und Jünglinge besseren Standes trugen den mit zwei langen, bis zum Handgelenk reichenden Aermel versehenen Leibrock (χιτὼν χειριδωτός). . . ." In support of this declaration he refers to a statement made by Hesychius (a very late authority), to the

Greeks as barbaric and the *tunica manicata*[1] was considered effeminate by the Romans down to the later Empire is interesting as bearing on the date of the miniatures (see pp. 9 ff.).

In C, the colour[2] used for the tunics of young men and old men is bluish- or grayish-white (*caeruleus:* Weston, 39); for the *pallia* yellow[3] (*flavus*) is employed. In F, the colours of the garments of young men, old men, and women vary.

The foot-gear of the miniatures varies according to the MSS. in which it is found, rather than according to the characters represented, except that

---

effect that the ἀμφιμάσχαλος χιτὼν χειριδωτός was worn by freemen, to certain ancient representations of comic scenes (Abb. 910–912), and to the article *Chiton* in Baumeister. The description of the ἀμφιμάσχαλος χιτών given in Baumeister, 380 B, is different from that given by Hesychius, *l.c.*, and more in harmony with that given in Smith, Dictionary of Antiquities, 1. 814, *s.v. Exomis*. Again, in Baumeister, 380 B, the essentially un-Hellenic character of the long-sleeved tunic is emphasized. In connection with Abb. 910–912, relied on by Baumeister to support his statement quoted above, see his own descriptions on p. 828 and the literature there cited; these representations all belong to a time much later than the best period of the Roman theatre. See also below, p. 82, n. 1; p. 83.

[1] See Smith, Dictionary of Greek and Roman Antiquities,[3] 2. 120. Cf. Verg. Aen. 9. 619; Cic. 2 Cat. 10; Gellius, 7. 12; August. De Doct. Christ. 3. 20.

[2] Bethe, 10, 20.

[3] Weston (Harvard Studies, 14. 39) states that the over-garments of young men in C are brownish-red or blue.

always in F and in all the examples of C and P at my command the women are not represented with shoes — in fact, often the feet do not show at all.

From O I have only two examples of women: (1) Thais Meretrix (Eun. 771), who wears a low sort of slipper like those of the men around her, and (2) Sophrona Nutrix (Ph. 728), whose low slippers are not ornamented alike.

Generally speaking, in C all male characters wear what seems to be a sole with straps crossed over the foot and up to and above the ankle. The point of fastening of the straps, if it shows at all, is in the back.[1] In P the shoe is low, with straps around the front part of the foot from under the sole and extending sometimes a little way up the leg. In F all feet are more or less indistinct, no shoes being seen save at

(1) Eun. 771, where Thraso Miles seems to have high boots. This is also possibly true of one of his assistants in the mock siege. See below, pp. 83, 117.

(2) Hec. 769, where the figure of Laches Senex shows thongs around and above the ankle.

(3) Ph. 348 and 591, where Geta Servus shows shoe-latchets, fastened in the back, at the ankle.

---

[1] Exceptional is one of Syrus's shoes, Ad. 364½.

In O, the few examples at my command show, generally, a low slipper.

Engelhardt's opinion [1] of the foot-gear in C and P is worth quoting for its bearing on the date of the miniatures: "Aehnliche Fussbekleidungen finden sich zwar in Griechenland, haben aber wahrscheinlich nicht zur Bühnenbekleidung gehört, denn sie finden sich nicht auf den Komödiendarstellungen griechischen Ursprungs und kamen auch in Rom in ähnlicher Form zur Verwendung, aber selten; öfter dagegen findet sich diese Art der Fussbekleidung im germanischen Gebiet, aber auch auf den frühchristlichen Denkmälern in Italien kommt sie vor."

### ANCILLA

The Ancilla appears once in the Amphitruo, Casina, Cistellaria, Menaechmi, Miles Gloriosus, Mostellaria, Persa, Andria, and Hautontimorumenos, and twice in the Stichus, Truculentus, and Eunuchus.

Two of Plautus's Ancillae are plainly old:

(1) From Mer. 671–677 we learn clearly that Syra Anus, the Ancilla of Dorippa Mulier, is eighty-four years old; she walks too slowly to keep up with her mistress, who, to be sure, is somewhat excited (666–669); she is carrying

[1] Die Illustrationen der Terenzhandschriften, 52 ff.

branches of laurel which Dorippa is to present to Apollo — possibly some other burdens also.

(2) Scapha, the Ancilla of Philematium Meretrix, who is assisting her mistress at her toilet, is no longer young, for she says (Mo. 199–201):

> vides quae sim: et quae fui ante.
> . . . atque uni modo gessi morem,
> qui pol me, ubi aetate hoc caput colorem commutavit,
> reliquit deseruitque me.

For this declaration she has paved the way by her words at 194–196.

The general impression which we get of the other Ancillae is that they are young. Milphidippa is *bellula* (Mi. 989). Stephanium has decked herself out for Stichus and Sagarinus Servi, to feast and dance with them (St. 742–744). The pert Astaphium, Ancilla of Phronesium Meretrix, excites the angry Stratulax not merely by her manner, but by the elaborate way in which she has got herself up. She wears a *pallula* of uncertain colour (Tru. 271), bronze armlets (Tru. 271–274), her hair is artificially curled[1] and elaborately dressed (Tru. 287), and her face is so covered with cosmetics that she has lost the power to blush (Tru. 290–294). She has also made plen-

---

[1] Cf. the criticism conveyed at times by *cincinnatus* (p. 46, n. 1).

tiful use of perfumes (Tru. 289).[1] The Ancilla of Erotium asks Menaechmus II to bring her some ear-rings (Men. 541–542).[2]

It would seem that there must have been something distinctive in the dress of an Ancilla, for, when Mysis appears before the house where the Andrian lives, Simo Senex (who, so far as we know, has never seen her before) asks (And. 461), *Ab Andria ancilla haec?* The main difference between the costume of the Ancilla and that of other women seems to lie in the greater simplicity of the former. In Juvenal 3. 93–95 we read:

> An melior cum Thaida sustinet, aut cum
> uxorem comoedus agit vel *Dorida nullo cultam palliolo?*[3]

Further, Pollux, at the end of his chapter on the Masks of the New Comedy (Onom. IV, 154), writes: ἡ δὲ ἄβρα περίκουρος θεραπαινιδιόν ἐστι περικεκαρμένον, χιτῶνι μόνῳ ὑπεζωσμένῳ λευκῷ χρώμενον. τὸ δὲ παράψηστον θεραπαινίδιον, διακέκριται τὰς τρίχας, ὑπόσιμόν τέ ἐστι καὶ δουλεύει ἑταίραις, ὑπεζω-

---

[1] On perfumes cf. Scapha's words to Philematium Meretrix (Mo. 273): Mulier recte olet ubi nil olet; *ibid.* 274–278; Martial 2. 12; 3. 63. 3–4; 6. 55. 5; 10. 72. 11. *Unguentatus* is often a term of reproach.

[2] For 'tips' to slaves, see, *e.g.*, As. 162 ff.; Hor. Serm. 1. 9. 57; Iuv. 3. 183–189.

[3] Cf. Martial, 9. 32. 1; 11. 27. 8.

σμένον χιτῶνα κοκκοβαφῆ. However, it is reasonable to suppose that the degree of simplicity varied with the taste and wealth of the mistress (see, *e.g.*, the description of Astaphium, the Ancilla of a Meretrix, pp. 53–54; cf. Pollux IV, 154, cited above).

### TESTIMONY OF THE MINIATURES

The sole miniatures of Ancillae at my command are two from C,[1] eight or nine from P,[2] and fifteen or sixteen from F.[2] These show a loose garment extending from the neck to the feet, generally with a girdle, and with flaring sleeves reaching to the elbow. Beneath these short sleeves are seen — once, perhaps twice, in C, generally in P, only twice in F[3] — other long sleeves much closer and reaching to the wrist (cf. the two sets of sleeves described under ADULESCENS, pp. 48 ff.). Regularly[4] in all three MSS. there are at least traces of a mantle over the left shoulder and down the left side, unless the left hand is engaged in gesticulation or in holding something.

---

[1] These are from Wieseler, Denkmäler, Tafel X, 2, 3.

[2] The identity of one Ancilla in P and of one in F is not certain.

[3] At Eun. 818 and 840.

[4] There is one exception in the examples from F (Eun. 668), one possible exception in those from P (And. 236), and one exception in the two examples from C (And. 236).

With this we may compare what is said below concerning the Servus and his scarf (see SERVUS, pp. 106–108). An interesting variation from the rule is seen in the picture of Mysis (And. 716, P), where both hands are employed in gesticulation and the mantle-ends are wound around both arms.

In P the hair is more or less dishevelled, with no trace of elaborate arrangement; in F it is rather elaborately puffed, but the ends are often flying from the shoulders. Once in F the puffing is omitted (Pythias, Eun. 1002); once (Eun. 923, F) the same character shows a high bow standing upright at the front of the part in her hair, and once (Eun. 727, F) it looks as if a corner of her mantle were put over her head. One of the two cases from C shows the hair parted in the centre, with the ends loose and flying; the other shows it rather elaborately dressed.

For the indistinct treatment of women's feet in all the MSS. see ADULESCENS, pp. 50–52.

### ANUS

This rôle is found in the Aulularia, Curculio, Mercator, Hautontimorumenos, Hecyra, and Adelphoe.

The plays give us little information about the Anus. Leaena Anus is a Lena in the Curculio, *multibiba atque merobiba* (Cu. 76),[1] an *anus tremula* (Cu. 160). Syra Anus Ancilla (Mer.) has already been treated under ANCILLA (p. 52). In the Hecyra (74–75), Syra Anus Lena, exhorting Philotis Meretrix against faithfulness to any particular lover, says:

> eheu me miseram, quor non aut istaec mihi
> aetas et formast aut tibi haec sententia!

Pollux writes thus of the costumes of old women in the New Comedy (Onom. IV, 119): ἡ μὲν τῶν γραῶν, μηλίνη, ἡ ἀερίνη, πλὴν ἱερειῶν. ταύταις δὲ λευκή.

### TESTIMONY OF THE MINIATURES

The five pictures of Anus[2] in my possession are all from F (I shall describe under NUTRIX, p. 85, the miniatures of Sophrona Nutrix at Phormio, 728, who is, however, designated as *Sophrona Anus* in C, P, and O). The five pictures show a long undergarment, with short, flowing sleeves, and a mantle arranged like a *pallium*.

Canthara Anus (Ad. 288, F) looks distinctly *not* old; in fact, of the five miniatures only that of Syra Anus at Hecyra, 58 (and possibly at vs.

---

[1] Canthara, the name of the Anus in Adelphoe, perhaps conveys the same suggestion (cf. *cantharus*).

[2] Haut. 614; Ad. 288, 299; Hec. 58, 75.

75) shows an old face. At verse 58 her hair is plainly done; at verse 75 it is less plainly dressed. The hair of Canthara in the Adelphoe (288 and 299, F) is puffed, as in the case of the Ancillae in F (p. 56). The remaining case, that of Canthara Anus[1] at Haut. 614, shows hair moderately puffed. This Canthara is slightly bent, and being rather short, looks almost deformed.

For the face and hair of the Anus cf. Pollux, Onom. IV, 150–151.

### COCUS

The Cocus appears twice in the Aulularia and once in the Casina, Curculio, Menaechmi, Mercator, Miles Gloriosus, Pseudolus, and Andria. Sometimes he is a slave (Au. 310; Men. 300), sometimes a freedman (And. 35).

In the Aulularia we see that cooks were frequently hired for special occasions, as we hire caterers, and that they brought their *vasa* with them (445–446; cf. below, Mer. 781).[2] When Congrio Cocus has been beaten and is fleeing from Euclio's house, the old man calls after him, threatening to bring him before the *tresviri* (416–

---

[1] The picture is, however, designated simply *Nutrix*.

[2] Cf. Middleton and Mills, Student's Companion to Latin Authors, 14; Rankin, The Rôle of the Μάγειροι in the Life of the Ancient Greeks, etc. (1907).

417); whereupon the cook asks *quamobrem?* Euclio answers, *quia cultrum habes.* To this Congrio rejoins *cocum decet.* So Cario Cocus has a knife in Mi. 1397, 1406–1408.

In the Menaechmi, as elsewhere, the *obsonium* is associated with the cook. Erotium Meretrix is to entertain Menaechmus I and his parasite at dinner; so she sends Cylindrus Cocus to do the marketing (219 ff.):

(Er.) *Sportulam* cape atque *argentum:* eccos *treis nummos* habes.
(Cy.) Habeo. (Er.) Abi atque *obsonium* adfer. tribus vide quod sit satis.

In verse 273 he returns from the market, bringing the *obsonium* (cf. 320, 326, 330).

In the Mercator, Lysimachus Senex buys the provisions (754), but the cook and his assistants seem to deliver them (778–780). Presently (781) the *vasa* are referred to as if they belonged to the Cocus (cf. Au. 445–446).

The Andria opens with directions from Simo Senex to his slaves, apparently, and then to his cook, the freedman, Sosia (1 ff.):

Vos istaec intro auferte: abite. Sosia,
adesdum: paucis te volo.

The answering words of Sosia suggest that *istaec* must be the *obsonium.*

The cook's apron is referred to by Pollux, Onom. IV, 119: Τῷ δὲ μαγείρῳ, διπλῆ, ἄγναπτος ἡ ἐσθής.

### TESTIMONY OF THE MINIATURES

Especially interesting are the pictures of the scene of the Andria just alluded to. They are found in C, P, and O.[1] In all three miniatures the costume of Sosia, who is, by the way, a *libertus*, is not distinguishable from that of the two attending slaves. He wears a short tunic, girded at the waist, with long, close sleeves; in C and P there are small, dark, rectangular patches just above the knees, and in C similar patches are seen on the sleeves close to the shoulder (cf. MILES, p. 82). In O his tunic is striped horizontally and ornamented with a border [2] around the bottom and the neck. He carries something which in C and O — and, less clearly, in P — is a spoon.[3] In all three MSS. the attendant nearest Sosia carries an *amphora* on his left shoulder; in C and P he has one large bird in the right hand, in O two birds on a stick over the right shoulder. In all three MSS., again, the second attendant has

---

[1] The Andria is entirely lacking in F.

[2] This border is not unusual in the garments shown by O.

[3] Cf. Wieseler, Denkmäler, 71 b.

three fish hanging from a ring in the right hand, while over the left shoulder C and P show a branch, and O a large bunch of some vegetable growth.

## LENA

In three of the five instances of the occurrence of this rôle[1] one common feature is observable: the women are old, or, at least, no longer young. From Asinaria 539 we may fairly infer that Cleareta has gray hair, for she says:

meum caput contemples, siquidem ex re consultas tua.

The Lena of the Curculio — *multibiba atque merobiba*, an *anus tremula* — has already been treated under ANUS (pp. 56–57), as has Syra Anus Lena of the Hecyra, who wishes (74–75) that she had Philotis's youth and beauty, or that Philotis had her wisdom (p. 57).

In Onomasticon IV, 120 Pollux writes: Αἱ δὲ μαστροποὶ, ἢ μητέρες ἑταιρῶν, ταινίδιόν τι πορφυροῦν περὶ τὴν κεφαλὴν ἔχουσιν.

Wieseler, in his Denkmäler (Taf. XI, 4), reproduces a wall-painting from Herculaneum which represents a scene from comedy, in which a slave is addressing two women, presumably a

---

[1] It occurs once in the Asinaria, Curculio, and Hecyra, and twice in the Cistellaria.

*meretrix* and a *lena.* The latter is described by Helbig[1] as follows: "mit rothem Kopftuch, in hellgrünem Chiton, einen ziegelrothen Mantel über dem linken Arme."

### TESTIMONY OF THE MINIATURES

The sole miniatures of the Lena at my command are the two of Syra Anus Lena already described under ANUS (pp. 57–58). I there called attention to the fact that the only pictures of the Anus which really show an old face are the two of this woman (Hec. 58 and 75), who has the additional designation, *Lena.* According to the evidence of the plays themselves, the idea of age seems to have been associated with *lenae;* was this idea, we may ask, so pronounced and so inevitably connected with *lenae* (rather than with the *anus,* specifically so called) that it gained expression in the miniatures in the case of Syra Anus *Lena,* but not in the case of Canthara Anus, either in the Hauton or the Phormio (if, indeed, Sophrona of the Phormio is to be considered among the Anus: see p. 85). Such a suggestion is hardly probable; a better reason for the older, less attractive, appearance of Canthara Anus Lena may be found in the fact that her somewhat

[1] Campanische Wandgemälde, 354 ff.

derogatory remark about her own appearance occurs in the very first scene (74–75), just before the second of the two miniatures in question, and only seventeen lines beyond the first.

## LENO

The casual reader of Plautus will be surprised to find that the rôle of Leno [1] is not a very frequent one, so strong is his impression to the contrary. This impression is, doubtless, due to the fact that the poet has done some particularly good character-drawing in connection with his Lenones, and that the appearance of three of the five is quite fully described.

The first Leno whom we meet is Cappadox, described as follows by a slave in the Curculio (230–233):

> quis hic est homo
> *cum collativo ventre* atque *oculis herbeis?*
> *de forma novi: de colore* non queo
> novisse. iamiam novi: lenost Cappodox.

Only that part of the description which is *de forma* is of value to us, for the unusual *color* and the *oculi herbei* seem to have been due to an attack

---

[1] The Leno appears once in each of the following plays of Plautus, Cur., Per., Poe., Ps., Ru., once also in the Phormio and the Adelphoe.

of jaundice (cf. 216–222), and are, therefore, purely incidental.

The Leno of the Persa is more briefly described, but we get here one or two points which are fairly typical. For example, Dordalus carries a *scipio* (816), which suggests the passage in Pollux, Onom. IV, 120,[1] where the straight staff, the attribute of the Leno, is mentioned along with his costume. Again, Dordalus has a *crumina*,[2] as one might expect of a man who is always receiving money in the conventional New Comedy. Moreover, we see a similar use of the *marsuppium* by Lycus Leno (Poe. 782–784).

That the typical Leno was ugly in appearance comes out particularly well in the case of this same Lycus. In Poe. 613, where an Advocatus and a Vilicus are talking together, Lycus appears, whereupon the Advocatus says (613)

> illic homost qui egreditur leno,

and the steward retorts:

> bonus est, *nam similis malist.*

Of the three Lenones who are most fully de-

---

[1] Πορνοβοσκοὶ δὲ χιτῶνι βαπτῷ καὶ ἀνθεινῷ περιβολαίῳ ἐνδέδυνται, καὶ ῥάβδον εὐθεῖαν φέρουσιν· ἄρεσκος καλεῖται ἥδε ἡ ῥάβδος. Contrast with this straight staff the curved staff of the Senex (pp. 96, 98).

[2] Cf. Ballio, Leno of the Pseudolus, below (p. 65).

scribed, two are stout (see Cur. 231, Ru. 317), but Ballio of the Pseudolus is thin — *nam hunc fames iam occiderit* (350). He has a peculiar sidewise walk (954–955):

illuc sis vide,
ut transvorsus, non provorsus cedit, quasi cancer solet.

Simia declares (980) that he is dressed like a housebreaker. As he goes to market, a Puer carries his *crumina* (170). Quite peculiar to this Leno is the *terginum* (154–155) or rawhide,[1] with which he encourages the unwilling obedience of his Lorarii (see p. 69).

Of the three Lenones already referred to as being most fully described two have beards, Ballio's being characterized as *hirquina barba* (Ps. 967). In the case of Labrax Leno the beard is barely mentioned (Ru. 769), but to his hair reference is often made: hominem *crispum, incanum* (125), *recalvom* ad Silanum senem (317), di te amant *cum inraso capite* (1303). His generally unpleasant appearance is suggested in verse 126 and clearly indicated in lines 317–319:

recalvom ad Silanum senem, statutum, ventriosum,
tortis superciliis, contracta fronte, fraudulentum,
deorum odium atque hominum, malum, mali viti
probrique plenum.

[1] At least, it is not mentioned in connection with other Lenones.

Labrax is the single instance in the plays from which we get information about the clothing of the Leno. He comes to land after the shipwreck, wet and scantily clothed (Ru. 488, 528). His traveller's *vidulus,* containing all his money (545–546), has gone to the bottom; the one tunic and the *pallium*[1] which he wears are all that is left to him (549–550):

Eheu! redactus sum usque ad *unam hanc tuniculam*
et ad *hoc misellum pallium:* perii oppido.

That the Leno's *pallium* was regularly particoloured is the statement of Donatus, De Com. VIII, 6: *leno pallio colore vario utitur.* Compare with this the statement of Pollux already cited (p. 64, n. 1; see also p. 43, n. 2).

### TESTIMONY OF THE MINIATURES

I have had access to the following miniatures of Terence's two Lenones — three of Sannio from F (Ad. 155, 209, 265) and one of Dorio (Ph. 485) from each of the chief illustrated MSS., C, P, F, and O. All show a tunic with close, long sleeves; only one (Ad. 155) shows a *pallium* in its conventional form.

---

[1] He must have started on his journey in these garments, for there was no chance to change them after sailing. See note on the traveller, p. 46, n. 2.

Most interesting in view of the περιβόλαιον mentioned by Pollux (see p. 64, n. 1) are the pictures of Dorio at verse 485 of the Phormio. In P, F, and O his mantle fastens down the middle of the front; it is sleeveless but of sufficient width to cover the left arm and to extend well over the right shoulder. The mantle is open on the right side, allowing free play to the right arm. In C the front seam of Dorio's cloak (which is otherwise like the one just described) does not appear. In F its right-hand side is marked by straight edges and square corner, but in C, P, and O the lines are more pleasing.

The two remaining pictures of Sannio (Ad. 209, 265, F) show a sleeveless and seamless mantle which must have been put on over the head. Again, its width is sufficient to extend beyond the shoulder down upon the arm. The front is pointed and hangs in folds from both sides to the centre.

Several of these miniatures show the Leno as somewhat bald (cf. Ru. 317).

### LORARIUS

This is a fairly common rôle in Plautus,[1] though it appears only once, with certainty, in Terence — viz. in the Andria.

---

[1] There is a Lorarius in the Bacchides and the Captivi, and there are Lorarii in the following plays: Mer., Mi., Mo., Ps., Ru.

The function of the Lorarius is defined in the following words from Gellius (10. 3. 19): itaque hi sequebantur magistratus, tamquam in scaenicis fabulis qui dicebantur lorarii, et quos erant iussi vinciebant aut verberabant.

One would naturally expect the *lora* to be the symbol of the Lorarius. There are numerous places where we may infer that he has *lora, restes, fustes,* or *manicae* (Ba. 799, 809, 811, 861–862; Cap. 200–201, 659, 667; Mi. 1401 a, 1403–1406, 1418, 1424; Ru. 816); in verse 1064 of the Mostellaria we can be practically sure that the *manicae* were on the stage. In the Rudens a Lorarius is ordered to bring *clavae* (798–799), one of which he gives to a second Lorarius; both then stand guard over Labrax Leno (809–812). The word *clava* appears to be used synonymously with *fustis* (816, 823).

That the Lorarii did not form a special class of slaves, but that they were ordinary household slaves who might be detailed to this kind of work has been clearly stated by Lorenz in his introductory note on the scene in the Mostellaria beginning with verse 1064. Two plays confirm this position particularly well.

(1) The Mercator (277–283), where the Lorarius is a common slave who carries *rastri* out to the *vilicus* on his master's farm and gives a message to his master's wife.

(2) The Pseudolus (154 ff.), where Ballio Leno strikes the sleepy (143) Lorarii with his raw-hide and then proceeds to give to five of them such directions as might be given to any slaves. One, who has an *urna* (157), is told to bring water for the cook; a second, who has a dull axe (158–159), is commanded to attend to the supply of wood, and common, household tasks — cleaning the house, spreading the couches, washing the plate (161–164) — are assigned to three others.

In the Andria, again, we find a Lorarius who is what we should expect a Lorarius to be (see 860–865), but the text does not necessarily imply that any instruments of torture are visible on the stage. Moreover, Dromo Lorarius of the miniature at 842 in O (this picture is lacking in C, P, and F) is in no way to be distinguished from an ordinary Servus (see pp. 104–108).

### TESTIMONY OF THE MINIATURES

I have examined but one miniature which is certainly that of a Lorarius — the picture in O just referred to, of Dromo, at verse 842 of the Andria. He wears a long-sleeved tunic, and grasps with his left hand the usual scarf of the Servus (see pp. 106–108).

In no other play of Terence do we find a Lorarius among the Dramatis Personae, but the miniatures in C, P, F, and O assign that designation to Donax at Eun. 771. The names of the besieging party are badly confused in all four pictures, but Donax must be the slave who has the crowbar (774), just as Sanga is the one with the *peniculus* (776–778). There is nothing in the dress of either to distinguish him from other Servi (see pp. 104–108).

### MATRONA, MULIER, UXOR

From the plays themselves we get no information concerning the details of the regular costume of the Matrona, the Mulier, and the Uxor. Moreover, the three types themselves are confused and obviously overlap one another. The Matrona of the Dramatis Personae of the *fabulae palliatae* of Plautus and Terence is, of course, not the Roman matron, whose distinguishing marks were the *stola* and the *instita* and her peculiar way of dressing her hair.[1]

Some of the Matronae are neither amiable nor attractive. The wife of Menaechmus I is repeatedly characterized as 'cross' (*tristis;* see Men. 607–608, 622, 644, 777; cf. also Men. 110 ff.), though it must be admitted that her state is quite

[1] See Smith's Dictionary of Greek and Roman Antiquities, 1. 500 ff., under *Coma;* 2. 717 ff., under *Stola.* Cf. also Lorenz, Mostellaria, Excurs zu vss. 224–226; p. 75 below.

justifiable in view of the situation. Sostrata's husband calls her a *mulier odiosa* (Haut. 1006) and asks her (1006–1008):

> ullam ego rem umquam in vita mea
> volui, quin tu in ea re mihi advorsatrix fueris, Sostrata?

Of their son he says (1020–1021):

> nam tui similis est probe.
> nam illi nil vitist relictum, quin idem itidem sit tibi.

Pollux, writing of the costume of women in Comedy, says (Onom. IV, 120): Ἡ δὲ τῶν νέων, λευκὴ ἢ βυσσίνη. Ἐπικλήρων δὲ, λευκὴ, κροσσωτή.

TESTIMONY OF THE MINIATURES

I have had access to twenty miniatures of Matronae and Mulieres — two from C, three from P, one from O, and the remaining fourteen from F. The one from O (of Nausistrata Mulier, Ph. 784) shows a long undergarment with long, flowing sleeves ornamented with a border.[1] There are traces, too, of a border on the skirt. There is no mantle.

In the remaining MSS. the representations of these three types of women show a long undergarment, sometimes the two sets of sleeves already so often described, less often the one set

---

[1] It will be remembered that this border is a characteristic feature of the miniatures in O. See p. 60, n. 2.

of sleeves, short and flowing.[1] There is a mantle which follows the general lines of a *pallium* and not infrequently is so arranged as to pass over the head in folds.[2] When the hair shows, it is commonly arranged with considerable care.

These observations serve to confirm what Wieseler[3] wrote more than half a century ago of the miniatures which he had examined: "In Betreff der Tracht der weiblichen Personen findet man im Allgemeinen eine Confusion, wie sie sich bei den männlichen nicht in dem Grade zeigt." The only invariable distinction which I have been able to make between the costumes of Ancilla, Anus, Matrona, Mulier, and Uxor is that the Anus never has long sleeves; but even this is probably quite accidental and due to the fact that only five pictures of the Anus were available.

### MERETRIX

This rôle is one of the commonest in both Plautus and Terence, occurring once in the Asi-

---

[1] Unusual is the single set of *long* sleeves worn by Sostrata (Hec. 243, F); they are close at the wrist, increasing in size towards the shoulder. It is easy to see how an artist may have carelessly altered the ordinary double sleeve of the miniatures (pp. 48 ff.) to something like this.

[2] This is never true of an Ancilla or Anus, with the possible exception of Pythias Ancilla, Eun. 727, F.

[3] Denkmäler, 76 b.

naria, Menaechmi, Mercator, Miles Gloriosus, Persa, Truculentus, Hautontimorumenos, Eunuchus, and Adelphoe, and twice in the Bacchides, Cistellaria, Mostellaria, and Hecyra. In Pseudolus 172 ff. several Meretrices appear as *mutae personae.*

The most prominent characteristic of the Meretrix is her beauty. She is *bella specie* (Ba. 838), *tam lepida* (Ba. 1169), *bella* (Ba. 1172), *lepida forma, forma eximia* (Mer. 13), *scita forma* (Mer., Arg. I, 2), *pulcra* (Poe. 1182, 1193), *mulier qua mulier alia nullast pulcrior* (Mer. 101), while Agorastocles Adulescens says of his Adelphium (Poe. 277–278), *nam Venus non est Venus: hanc equidem Venerem venerabor,* etc., and the Senex, Lysimachus, who is presumably less impressionable than the typical Adulescens, bids Pasicompsa cease her weeping lest she spoil her lovely eyes (Mer. 501).

The exigencies of a particular plot may require a Meretrix to neglect her personal appearance, as in the case of the sorrowful Selenium of the Cistellaria[1]; but she is, normally, elaborately gotten up (*exornata:* see TERMINOLOGY, pp. 25–26) and the excessive care bestowed upon her toilet is repeatedly emphasized. Notable examples of this

[1] Cf. Ci. 113–114: (Gy.) . . . : sicine immunda, obsecro, ibis? (Sel.) Immundas fortunas aequomst squalorem sequi.

are Poe. 210–232 and the entire third scene of Mostellaria, Act I (159–312), where Philematium discusses her toilet with her maid, calling for cosmetics (*cerussa* and *purpurissum*, 258–264), asking how her hair looks (254),

> suo quique loco? viden? capillus satis compositust commode?

and how her *palla* becomes her (282), and trying the effect of her trinkets, which are referred to indiscriminately as *aurum* (282) and *ornamenta* (248, 294).[1] Interesting in this connection is the passage in the Epidicus (213 ff.) where Epidicus Servus describes the crowd of Meretrices whom he saw in the streets of Athens,[2] hurrying to greet their soldier-*amatores* just returned from a campaign which had taken them to Thebes or its neighbourhood.

In the Miles Gloriosus, where the disguise of Philocomasium Meretrix as the wife of Periplecomenes Senex is planned, Palaestrio Servus says (Mi. 791–792):

> itaque eam huc ornatam adducas: ex matronarum modo,
> capite compto, crinis vittasque habeat adsimuletque se tuam esse uxorem.

---

[1] See TERMINOLOGY, p. 20.

[2] For Ep. 217 I accept Lindsay's text *quom ad portam venio;* this text rests on the MSS. and emendation to *portum* is needless.

When Acroteleutium appears presently on the stage (871–872), to carry out this plan, Palaestrio exclaims significantly:

> quam digne ornata incedit, ⟨h⟩aud meretricie!

Cf. Lorenz's[1] comments: "Acroteleutium, die hübsche junge Klientin des Periplecomenes im ornatus matronarum! Züchtig drapiert sie sich in das lange, weisse und faltenreiche Gewand der römischen Hausfrau, und das sonst wohl ganz anders kokett frisierte Haar ist bescheiden in die sechs schlichten Flechten geteilt, die in Rom das *insigne pudoris der honestae feminae* bildeten." We have here, then, a distinctly Roman touch. Contrast what was said above (p. 70) concerning the Matrona as one of the Dramatis Personae of the *fabulae palliatae.*

Only a few times is mention made in the plays of the individual garments of the Meretrix. Selenium, about to leave the house, is told to hold up her *amiculum* (Ci. 115), which is dragging; Adelphasium, too, seems to be wearing an *amiculum.* In the Mostellaria, Philematium, who is adorning herself to please her lover, says to her maid (282):

> agedum contempla aurum et *pallam,*[2] satin haec ⟨me⟩
> deceat.

---

[1] Einleitung zum Miles Gloriosus, 21.

[2] Cf. the *palla* which Menaechmus I stole from his wife in order to present it to Erotium Meretrix (Men. Act I. 3).

In the Truculentus Phronesium bids her maid throw a *pallium* (479) over her, as she reclines, and in the next scene she receives, as a present from Stratophanes Miles, a *pallula ex Phrygia* (536). She wears *soleae* on her feet (479, 631). Wieseler[1] cites the following passage from Varro in Meleagris (302), quoted by Nonius (under the words *tunica* and *demittere:* see Lindsay, 2. 442; 3. 861 = 286 M.; 536 M.): cum etiam *Thais Menandri tunicam demissam* habeat ad talos. He then proceeds to reconcile it with another selection from Nonius[2]: Meretrices apud veteres *subcinctiore veste* utebantur. Afranius Excepto "meretrix *cum veste longa?*" — "peregrino in loco solent tutandi causa sese sumere." Wieseler's explanation of the apparent inconsistency between these passages is that in the latter Roman usage is referred to, since Afranius was a writer of *togatae.* Likewise, the *toga meretricia* (Hor. Serm. 1. 2. 63; Mart. 2. 39, 10. 52; etc.) was *Roman,* not Greek.

In enumerating the colours worn by different characters, Donatus (De Com. VIII, 6) writes: meretrici ob avaritiam *luteum* datur (for Wieseler's doubt on this subject, see his Denkmäler, 79 b).

---

[1] Denkmäler, 76 b.
[2] Lindsay's Nonius 3. 868 = 541 M.

## TESTIMONY OF THE MINIATURES

In C, P, and O there are six pictures of Meretrices, all of which show a diadem [1] over the hair, which is seldom plainly dressed. In C and P we find a long undergarment and the double set of sleeves described under ADULESCENS and already referred to so often in connection with the miniatures. In O, the only example is Thais, at Eun. 771, who shows, curiously enough, one long, close sleeve and one shorter, flowing sleeve. With this one exception from O and one from P (Eun. 81), the Meretrix wears, in the three MSS. mentioned, a mantle which follows the general line of a *pallium;* quite unique is the case of Thais at Eun. 454, P, where the long undergarment shows an ornamented stripe throughout its entire length, on either side of the front, and where there is the barest trace of a mantle.[2]

---

[1] See Pollux, Onom. IV, 153–154: Ἡ *δὲ διάχρυσος ἑταίρα πολὺν ἔχει τὸν χρυσὸν ἐπὶ τῇ κόμῃ. ἡ δὲ διάμιτρος ἑταίρα μίτρᾳ ποικίλῃ τὴν κεφαλὴν κατείληπται.* The *meretrix* in the wall-painting already referred to under LENA (pp. 61–62) is thus described by Helbig (p. 354, n. 1472): "Ein mit goldfarbigem Haarbande geschmücktes Mädchen, vermutlich eine Hetäre, in blaurothem langärmeligem Chiton und weissem Mantel."

[2] Engelhardt (49 ff.) compares this costume of Thais with that of Theodora in a fourth-century mosaic (Wilpert, Die Malereien der Katakomben Roms, Tafel $174_2$).

In the thirteen miniatures from F the diadem never appears. The hair is seldom plainly dressed; in three cases (Eun. 771; Haut. 381; Ad. 155) the outer garment is drawn up over the head, as it was in the case of the MATRONA (see p. 72). Sometimes the sleeves of the undergarment are short and flowing, though more often two sets of sleeves are seen, as in C and P. There are usually clear traces of a *pallium*-like mantle, the most doubtful case being that of Thais at Eun. 778, where, save for the two sets of sleeves, her costume is not distinguishable from that of the Ancilla in the same picture.

### MILES

The rôle occurs in the Bacchides, Curculio, Epidicus, Miles Gloriosus, Poenulus, Truculentus, and in the Eunuchus.

One of the most common attributes of the Miles is the *machaera*, which he carries in the following passages: Ba. 887; Cu. 567, 574, 632; Mi. 5, 1423; Tru. 506, 613, 627, 927–929.[1] The *clipeus* is referred to as belonging to the Miles, but in no place is he surely wearing it on the stage.[2] At the opening of the Miles Gloriosus,

---

[1] *Ferrum* of verse 929 seems to be synonymous with *machaera*.

[2] Cu. 574 is too corrupt to yield reliable evidence.

Pyrgopolinices, as he comes out on the stage, calls back, presumably to slaves:

Curate ut splendor *meo* sit *clipeo* clarior
quam solis radii esse olim quom sudumst solent.

Tri. 596, 719 and Tru. 506 should have considerable weight in this connection.

The garments worn by a soldier are mentioned in Mi. 1423,

de *tunica et chlamyde* et machaera nequid speres, non feres.

In fact, the *chlamys* is quite generally assigned to him (Ba. 887; Cu. 611, 632; Ep. 435–436). In the Mercator, where Charinus comes out equipped for an expedition (857–865)[1] in search of his mistress, or, as he says in another place (884), intending to go into exile, he thus addresses the audience (851–854):

apparatus sum, ut videtis. abicio superbiam:
egomet mihi comes, calator, equos, agaso, armiger:
egomet sum mihi imperator, idem egomet mihi oboedio:
egomet mihi fero quod usust.

Hearing that his love is found, he cries (910–912):

sed quin ornatum hunc reicio? heus aliquis actutum huc foras
exite, illinc *pallium* mihi ecferte. . . .
. . . puere, cape *c⟨h⟩lamydem* atque istic ⟨a⟩sta ilico.

[1] Cf. p. 42, with n. 1.

Then, when he is told that he may not see her yet, he says (921–927):

*c⟨h⟩lamydem* sumam denuo. . . . cape sis, puer, hoc *pallium* . . . *sonam* sustuli . . . iam *machaerast* in manu . . . tollo ampullam[1] atque hinc eo.

The colour of the soldier's chlamys is given by Donatus (De Com. VIII, 6): militi *chlamys purpurea* . . . inducitur (cf. the costume of the soldier in tragedy, Poll. Onom. IV, 116).

Therapontigonus Miles has an *anulus* (Cu. 346–347, 356, 360, 584), but that is due to the exigencies of the plot and has no necessary connection with his character as Miles. In Tru. 535, Stratophanes has a *perula*, which is probably due to his travels (cf. 954).[2]

The Miles *par excellence* is, of course, Pyrgopolinices of the Miles Gloriosus — boastful of his impossible feats of skill and daring, and conceited about his personal appearance. There is an abundance of phrases which describe him in a *general* way, probably satirically, as *tam pulcer* (59), *nimia pulcritudine* (998), *tam pulcrum et praeclarum virtute et forma ⟨et⟩ factis* (1042); but the

---

[1] For the importance of the *ampulla* to a person on a journey see Knapp, Class. Phil. 2. 296, n.; Smith, Dictionary of Greek and Roman Antiquities³, 1. 116, *s.v. Ampulla.*

[2] For the costume of the traveller see p. 46, n. 2.

specific allusions are, almost without exception, to his hair, which was artificially curled and perfumed (923),[1] was thick and heavy, and was designated by the high-sounding, epic term *caesaries*[1] (64, 768), the comic force of the picture being thus increased by a parody of descriptions of kings and tragic heroes. Interesting in this connection is the following passage from Pollux (Onom. IV, 147), where he is writing of the masks of the New Comedy: Τῷ δὲ ἐπισείστῳ στρατιώτῃ ὄντι καὶ ἀλαζόνι καὶ τὴν χροιὰν μέλανι καὶ τὴν κόμην ἐπισείονται αἱ τρίχες. ὥσπερ καὶ τῷ δευτέρῳ ἐπισείστῳ, ἁπαλωτέρῳ ὄντι, καὶ ξανθῷ τὴν κόμην.

### TESTIMONY OF THE MINIATURES

The sole Terentian Miles is Thraso of the Eunuchus. Of his costume the play tells us nothing, but I have had access to nine miniatures — one from C, three from P, four from F, and one from O. Three from F (1025, 1031, 1049) show the garments which are most nearly like what we should expect — a long-sleeved tunic, girt as high as the knees, and a chlamys fastening with a clasp on the right shoulder; the fourth picture from F (771) shows no chlamys, but the troublesome, double set of sleeves (similar to those described

---

[1] See on the epithet *cincinnatus*, p. 46, n. 1.

under ADULESCENS, p. 48) appears here, as in the corresponding illustrations in C and P. Like all the other pictures of the Miles at 771, the one in O shows the high-girt tunic and no mantle, but is unlike the other three in having only one set of sleeves — the long, close sleeves. In the two remaining miniatures from P (391 and 454) the same short tunic shows what is also noticeable at 771 in P, a dark, oblong patch above each knee; the *chlamys*, fastened around the neck in front, with a clasp, is thrown back over the shoulders.

All of the nine miniatures show more or less peculiar head-gear. The one from C (771) shows a high cylindrical turban, on which the ornamentation takes the form of encircling bands; the corresponding miniature from P shows a similar turban with less regular ornamentation, but in the other two from P (391 and 454) are seen stiff hats in which a high, cylindrical base is surmounted by a projecting, flat crown, producing the effect of an exaggerated mortar-board.[1] The one in O at 771 resembles a crown — a 'Federkranz,' says Engel-

[1] All of these cylindrical hats in C and P Engelhardt (p. 52) compares to the Mauerkrone in classical art, "die meist weibliche, selten männliche Figuren tragen, die aber stets göttliche Personen auszeichnet; an diese wird wohl hier nicht zu denken sein, oder aber sie ist in ganz missverstandener Weise verwendet und spricht so für eine recht späte Entstehung der Bilder." Cf. Wieseler, Denkmäler, 76 b.

hardt (p. 51). In all four pictures from F, however, an entirely different type appears, clearly the Phrygian cap. Now, the Phrygian cap is appropriately worn by the Eunuchus (see p. 125). Has, then, the artist of F confused the Miles and the Eunuchus, or has he deliberately given to Thraso, the *peregrinus*[1] (759), this Oriental head-covering? Wieseler[2] thinks that Thraso must actually have worn the *petasus* and cites, as proof that this was the regular head-gear of soldiers in *fabulae palliatae*, Ps. 735 and 1186. However, the reference is not altogether satisfactory, for a Cacula is there in question — the soldier's *servus*, not the Miles himself.

Where the hair shows in pictures of the Miles, it is not particularly long, but it is often very thick and rather bushy. In F the Miles has beard and moustache.[3]

The foot-gear of Thraso in C, P, and O is what is worn by the male characters of the respective

---

[1] Plautine costumes of *peregrini* are numerous: *tunica, zona, chlamys, causia* (Per. 154–157); *chlamys* (for a Spartan *soldier*, Poe. 600, 649–656, 770, 780, 801–802); *chlamys, machaera, petasus, tunica manuleata* (soldier's *servus*, Ps. 732–738, 963–964, 1184–1186); very large hat (Tri. 840, etc.); *machaera, clipeus?* (Stratophanes Miles, Tru. 506, 613, 927–929, 955). See, also, POENUS (UNUSUAL RÔLES, p. 134).

[2] Denkmäler, 76 b and 77 a. Cf. also Tafel XI, 2, for wall-painting showing a Miles.

[3] Cf. Bethe, Praefatio 52 ff.

miniatures, but in F, where few shoes are seen,[1] the boots of Thraso in *one* picture (Eun. 771) are noteworthy (see CACULA, p. 117).

### NUTRIX

The only Nutrix in Plautus is Giddenis of the Poenulus. Nothing is told us of her costume; for her height, complexion, etc., see POENA (p. 133). Terence has, among his Dramatis Personae, two Nutrices,[2] both named Sophrona, one in the Eunuchus, the other in the Phormio; Canthara Anus of the Hautontimorumenos is also called *nutrix* (617) and so designated in the picture of her in F at verse 614. From the plays themselves we get only one piece of information, and that relates to Sophrona of the Phormio (732):

Nam quae *haec anus* est, exanimata a fratre quae
egressast meo?

### TESTIMONY OF THE MINIATURES

I have had access to only one picture of Sophrona Nutrix in the Eunuchus — that occurring

---

[1] See ADULESCENS, p. 51.

[2] The Nutrix in Hec. 770 is a *persona muta*, if she appears at all. Engelhardt (78) says that she appears in the miniatures of C and P at 767. In F we may assume a false assignment of names, in which case the costume of the figure corresponding to the Nutrix of C and P is satisfactory.

at verse 911, in F. She wears a long under-garment with short, flowing sleeves and a *pallium*, one end of which is particularly long as it hangs from her left arm. Her hair is parted in the centre, puffed on the side, and hangs down her back.

Sophrona Nutrix of the Phormio is designated as *Sophrona Anus* in C, P, and O and as *Sophrona* in F, at verse 728. These are the only pictures which we have of her; *anus* of C, P, and O is easily explained by the close proximity of *haec anus* (732). In C, P, and F she wears a long under-garment, reaching to the feet, the double set of sleeves, already so often noted in the costume of men and women, and a *pallium*-like mantle, the long end of which hanging from her left arm is grasped by Chremes Senex. In O she wears a long undergarment, with unusually broad, flowing sleeves, and no mantle.

Canthara Anus of the Hautontimorumenos appears in the picture at verse 614, in F, under the designation *Nutrix*. For her costume and appearance see ANUS, p. 58.

### PARASITUS

This is a common[1] rôle in Latin Comedy and one of considerable importance — the parasite

---

[1] The rôle occurs in the following plays: As., Cap., Cu., Men., Mi., Per., Ru., St., Eun., Ph.

gives his name to two plays, the Curculio and the Phormio.

In the case of four parasites there is distinct mention of the *pallium*. In the Cap. 779 (cf. 789) Ergasilus gathers it up and hastens to deliver a message in the manner of the *servus currens*.[1] Curculio stakes his *pallium* (Cu. 355) against a ring at a game of dice. Some women, in love with Pyrgopolinices, catch Artotrogus by the *pallium* (Mi. 59), to ask him questions about the Miles. Gelasimus is a *parasitus egens cum veste unica* (St. 350), who has not a farthing to give away or to lend, who owns nothing *nisi hoc quod habeo pallium* (St. 257). Gnatho is a type of the sleek, prosperous, and well-dressed parasite (Eun. 232, 253). Pollux (Onom. IV, 119), writing of the Parasitus in comedy, says: οἱ δὲ παράσιτοι μελαίνῃ ἢ φαιᾷ (ἐσθῆτι ἐχρῶντο), πλὴν ἐν Σικυωνίῳ, λευκῇ, ὅτε μέλλει γαμεῖν ὁ παράσιτος.

The attributes of the Parasitus are also mentioned by Pollux in the following section (120): τοῖς δὲ παρασίτοις πρόσεστι καὶ στλεγγὶς καὶ λήκυθος. An interesting parallel to this statement is found in Plautus's Stichus (230), where the parasite, who is offering certain things for sale, includes his *robiginosam strigilim, ampullam rubidam.* Doubt-

[1] Cf. Donatus (De Com. VIII, 6): *parasiti cum intortis palliis veniunt.*

less typical, also, are the articles mentioned in the Persa (123–125):

> cynicum esse ⟨e⟩gentem oportet parasitum probe:
> ampullam, strigilem, scaphium, soccos, pallium,
> marsuppium habeat.

In his note on Mo. 653 Lorenz, objecting to *adulescens* as applied to a Danista, includes in the same category parasites to whom the epithet is applied in the plays — as Peniculus (Men. 494) and Phormio (Ph. 378).[1] The idea of age seems to me by no means a necessary one in connection with a Parasitus; furthermore, it is not without significance that Pollux, in describing the masks[2] of the New Comedy, places the παράσιτος not with the γέροντες, but with the νεανίσκοι (Onom. IV, 146–148), and mentions more than one type of παράσιτος.[3]

---

[1] Interesting is Wieseler's treatment (Denkmäler, 79 b, 80 a) of the following passage from Ausonius, Epp. 23. 9–10:

> Canus, comosus, hispidus, trux, attubus,
> Terentianus Phormio.

[2] Even before the introduction of masks, the make-up may have had the same general features which it had in the later period.

[3] Wieseler, Denkmäler, 75 b, cites in this connection a passage from Athenaeus (VI, p. 237 b): παρασίτων δ' εἶναί φησι γένη δύο Ἄλεξις ἐν Κυβερνήτῃ (Fr. 1, Meineke's Fragm. Com. Gr. 3. 433 ff.) διὰ τούτων Δύ' ἐστί, Ναυσίνικε, παρασίτων γένη, ἓν μὲν τὸ κοινὸν καὶ κεκωμῳδημένον, οἱ μέλανες ἡμεῖς. N. θάτερον ζητῶ γένος. A. σατράπας παρασίτους καὶ στρατηγοὺς ἐπιφανεῖς, σεμνοπαράσιτον ἐκ μέσου καλούμενον, ὑποκρινό-

Curculio is several times referred to as one-eyed.[1] In verses 394–396 he explains how he lost his eye in a siege, but the explanation may well have been invented to give excuse for a device that would obviously help his disguise. Similarly, Pleusicles, disguised as a shipmaster (Mi. 1430), wears *scutulam ob oculos laneam,* which he explains in verses 1306–1310.

### TESTIMONY OF THE MINIATURES

I have had access to twenty-nine miniatures of the two Terentian Parasiti, Gnatho and Phormio. Of these, seven were from C, ten from P, seven from F, and five from O. It is so evident that the names are misplaced in the pictures of all four MSS. at Eun. 771 that it will be best to omit them from our reckoning at present and to consider first the remaining twenty-five miniatures.

The four pictures in O show the long-sleeved undergarment, raised rather high on one side, and the *chlamys*-like mantle. The twenty-one pictures from C, P, and F are fairly uniform in showing the long undergarment and two sets of sleeves[2] as

---

μενον εὖ τοῖς βίοις, ὀφρῦς ἔχον χιλιοταλάντους ἀνακυλῖόν τ' οὐσίας.

[1] *Unocule,* Cu. 392; *lusce,* Cu. 505, 543, 546: cf., however, Diomedes, Gram. Lat. 1. 489 (K).

[2] In C, at Ph. 829, and in P, at 990, the close undersleeve has not been finished.

described under ADULESCENS (pp. 48–49), with the familiar *pallium.*[1]

If, now, we return to the four troublesome miniatures at Eun. 771, two courses are open to us. We may accept for Gnatho the figure that is so designated in P, O, and F — the extreme left-hand figure, dressed in long, straight tunic with close, long sleeves, and grasping with both hands a scarf that passes around the body at the waist, a figure which we should naturally describe as that of a Servus. Or, we may hold, with Wieseler,[2] that the figure at Thais's right is Gnatho. This figure shows the long undergarment and two sets of sleeves as noted above, and the familiar *pallium;* thus it agrees admirably with the general type of Parasitus in the twenty-one unmistakable pictures from C, P, and F.

The latter theory is helped by the fact that in P and O the figure in question carries uplifted in his right hand a plume-like object similar to that which Phormio carries at verse 841 in C, P, and O. The identity of this instrument is not clear. Wieseler suggests[3] that it may be a sort of strigil, but he is rather inclined to believe that the artist

---

[1] In F, Eun. 1025, the mantle is *chlamys*-like.

[2] Denkmäler, 63 b, 67 a.

[3] *Ibid.*, 70 b, 71 a. Cf. above, pp. 86–87.

has referred to Phormio the action belonging to Antipho in verses 850–851,

(Ge.) Vapula. (An.) Id quidem tibi iam fiet, nisi resistis, verbero.
(Ge.) Familiorem oportet esse hunc: minitatur malum,

and has therefore represented Phormio, not Antipho, with an instrument[1] with which *minitatur malum.*

### PUER

This rôle is fairly common in Plautus[2]; in Terence, however, it occurs only once, in the Adelphoe.

The Puer seems to be an ordinary slave. In the Bacchides he attends a Parasitus (573, etc.); in the Captivi he gives directions to the *servi* and starts to find his master (918); in the Miles Lurcio Puer has been sent on an errand by Philocomasium Mulier (864), while another Puer summons Pyrgopolinices Miles to go to his love (1378 ff.). Sphaerio Puer seems to be bearing messages to and from Tranio Servus in behalf of an Adulescens (Mo. 409–430). In the Persa Paegnium Puer carries *tabellae* and messages to a Meretrix at the bidding

---

[1] See Scheffer, De Re Vehiculari, 1, ch. XIV, 196. The *flagella ex marmoribus veteribus ludorum Circensium expressa* resemble Phormio's instrument very perceptibly.

[2] It occurs in the following plays: Ba., Cap., Mi. (twice), Mo. (twice), Per., Poe., Ps., St.

of Toxilus Servus; this Puer is small (231, 848), young and handsome (229–230; cf. 276). The Puer of the Poenulus is apparently a Carthaginian slave, who proves to be the son of Giddenis Nutrix (Poe. 1140, etc.). The Leno of the Pseudolus, on his way to market, seems by his address to the Puer (170) to imply that the latter carries his master's *crumina.* Again, a Puer of this Leno refers to himself as *parvolus* for a certain kind of punishment (783).

In contrast with the general impression of the Puer as a subordinate slave-of-all-work, we find in the Stichus Pinacium Puer not merely working himself, but directing the other slaves in setting the house in order and preparing dinner for the return of the master (347–360). Pinacium had been sent to the harbour that morning by his mistress to inquire about incoming ships from Asia. Seeing his master aboard one, he hurried home eagerly (274–288) to tell the good news to the faithful wife. Pinacium is dressed as a Piscator might be (289, 317, 319–321) — he has rod, basket, and hook, and may have intended to fish while he lingered at the harbour on the watch for his master (see PISCATOR, p. 131).

The single Puer in Terence's Dramatis Personae is Dromo of the Adelphoe. In 375 ff. Syrus Servus calls to Dromo, who is not on the stage,

piscis ceteros purga, Dromo;
gongrum istum maxumum in aqua sinito ludere
tantisper.

A little farther on (380) Syrus calls to Stephanio (apparently another 'puer'),

salsamenta haec, Stephanio,
fac macerentur pulcre.

From the text we get no further description of the Puer, but the miniatures are interesting. P was not at my disposal for this passage, but Bethe gives C, F, and O for Ad. 364½ and F for 775. At 364½ all three MSS. show a male figure seated just inside a doorway, the other figures in the picture being outside. He wears a long-sleeved tunic, girt to the knee or higher, and a big-mouthed mask. He is dressing a fish, and one or two more lie close at hand. Near by is the eel (in O there are two eels) in a pot or bowl. At 775, where Dromo becomes one of the Dramatis Personae, F, the only MS. at my disposal for this passage, shows the grotesque-mouthed Dromo in a long-sleeved tunic, ankle-length, holding by the left hand the conventional scarf of the *Servus* (see SERVUS, pp. 106–108).

### SENEX

This role is found in all but four of Plautus's plays; in the Eunuchus it occurs once, in the

Andria and the Adelphoe three times, and in each of the other Terentian plays twice.

Though the term *senex*[1] may be applied to a man from the age of forty years upwards, the ordinary Senex of Latin Comedy must have been considerably above the minor limit. Periplecomenes (Mi. 629), to be sure, is not more than fifty-four, but Demipho (Mer. 524) is beyond sixty, and Menedemus (Haut. 62–63) is sixty or more. Furthermore, nothing is more frequently said of the Senex than that he is *cano capite* (As. 934; Ba. 1101, 1207–1208; Cas. 518; Mer. 305), *canus* (Cas. 238; Mer. 639), *capite candido* (Mo. 1148), or *albicapillus* (Mi. 631); cf. also *ad istanc capitis albitudinem* (Tri. 874). Gray's[2] interpretation of *defloccati* (Ep. 616) as 'shorn,' 'fleeced'[3] by the rascality of Epidicus seems more reasonable than the rendering 'bald'; but perhaps Epidicus is punning and intends to suggest both meanings. The father-in-law of Menaechmus I is *barbatus*[4] (Men. 854) and Nicobulus is *alba barba* (Ba. 1101). There are numerous other phrases which show that the Senex must have

---

[1] See Palmer's note on Am. 5. 1. 20 = 1072.

[2] See his edition of the Epidicus, *l.c.*

[3] So the Senes of the Bacchides are represented as *oves* (1121–1139) driven to the house of the Meretrices.

[4] Cf. Bethe, Praefatio, 53 ff.

been made up so as to look old: *istac aetate* (Ba. 1163; Mer. 972, 981–983; Mo. 1148), *istuc aetatis* (Mi. 618, 622), *senecta aetate* (Cas. 240), *haec mea senectus* (Tri. 381), *decrepitus* (Cas. 559; Mer. 291), *vetulus* (Ep. 187, 666), *edentulus* (Cas. 500; cf. Mer. 541), *tremulum* [1] (Men. 854), *Acheruntícus* (Mer. 290; cf. Mi. 626), *senex vetus* (Mer. 291), *vetus puer* (Mer. 976). Especially interesting is the use of *pater* applied to a Senex by a stranger (Mo. 952; Ru. 103; Tri. 878); it suggests the colloquial use of *uncle, grandfather*, in some sections of our own country.[2]

From the plays we get some good pictures of Senes.

(1) In the Casina we see Lysidamus, an old dandy, whose wife realizes his unfaithfulness and berates him thus (236–240):

unde hic, amabo, unguenta olent? (Ly.) Oh perii.
manufesto miser teneor. cesso caput pallio detergere?
ut te bonus Mercurius perdat, myropola, quia haec mihi dedisti.
(Cleo.) Eho tu, nili, cana culex: vix teneor, quin quae decent te dicam.
senecta aetate unguentatus [3] per vias, ignave, incedis?

---

[1] *Tremulum Tithonum*, though adopted by most editors, is not the reading of the MSS., which show instead *tremulum Titanum*. The latter reading is kept by Lindsay.

[2] Cf. *father*, Merchant of Venice, II. 2; see also Hor. Ep. 1. 6. 54 ff.

[3] Cf. p. 54, n. 1.

He is, further, *cano capite* (518), *edentulus* (550), and *decrepitus* (559).

(2) The father-in-law of Menaechmus I is thus referred to (Men. 853–854):

> hunc impurissimum
> barbatum, tremulum Tithonum,[1] qui cluet Cy⟨c⟩ino
> patre.

He has, too, a *scipio* (856).

(3) The sixty-year old Demipho, *cano capite*, strikes Lysimachus as being *Acheruntlcus, senex vetus, decrepitus* (Mer. 290–291), for the latter says scornfully of him (540–541):

> Puer est illequidem, stulta:
> nam illi quidem hau sane diust quom dentes exciderunt.

(4) This Lysimachus is one of the most absurd-looking of all the Senes (Mer. 639–640):

> canum, varum, ventriosum, bucculentum, breviculum,
> subnigris oculis, oblongis malis, pansam aliquantulum.

The old miser, Euclio, is rather slovenly (Au. 540); Callicles comes on in his working-clothes after digging up the treasure (Tri. 1099); Demea, finally, was doubtless dressed plainly, probably carelessly and in country fashion (Ad. 866).

In spite of the almost unanimous testimony of the miniatures, the plays themselves give us little information about the garments of the Senex.

---

[1] For this reading, see p. 94, n. 1.

Only in the Casina is he clearly wearing the *pallium* (237, 637, 945, 974–975, 978, 1009: in 246 we have *palliolum*), and nowhere do we hear of his tunic. From Donatus (De Com. VIII, 6) we learn that the clothing of Senes was white: comicis senibus *candidus vestis* inducitur, quod is antiquissimus fuisse memoratur.

The *scipio* is carried by Demaenetus (As. 124) and by the father-in-law of Menaechmus I (Men. 856). Lysidamus has lost his *scipio* (Cas. 975, 1009). The easy inference that Demea carries a staff (Ad. 571, 782) is not confirmed by the miniatures immediately preceding the respective scenes, not, at least, by the F miniatures, which alone are at my disposal; but at 713 in F (*defessus sum ambulando,* etc.) the artist has put in the *margin* a figure of Demea with a straight, smooth staff. The *fustes* which Euclio seems to have in the Aulularia (42, 422, 425, 440–443, 454, 632) and the *anulus* of Periplecomenes in the Miles (771, 797, 800) are not significant in their rôles as Senes.

That the Senex wore *socci* is a natural inference from Haut. 124,

> adsido: adcurrunt servi, *soccos* detrahunt.

A *marsuppium* is carried by Lysidamus (Cas. 490), and by Periphanes (Ep. 185); Charmides

Senex has lost his at sea [1] (Ru. 547–548). Some sort of money-bag Chremes (Haut. 831) and Demipho (Ph. 714–715) must have had, and so the miniatures [2] at my command represent them; similarly, Demea may have had a purse (Ad. 977), but the one miniature which I have examined shows none. The passage in Pollux (Onom. IV, 119) treating of the costume of old men in the New Comedy is corrupt; their masks are fully described in Onom. IV, 143–145.

### TESTIMONY OF THE MINIATURES

I have examined one hundred and fifty miniatures of the Senex, seventy-one from F, thirty-seven from P, twenty-four from C, and eighteen from O. There is a great uniformity in the costume of Senes in C, P, and F. The general type consists of a straight undergarment, reaching almost to the ankle, with two kinds of sleeve, visible as they were described under ADULESCENS (p. 48), and of a mantle of the usual *pallium*-style. The greatest variation in the manner of wearing the *pallium* is in F.[3] In O, strangely enough, the *chlamys* seems

---

[1] As a traveller, Charmides needed some sort of purse. See p. 46, n. 2.

[2] It is clear that in the miniatures of C preceding Ph. 714–715 the names of Demipho and Chremes have been interchanged.

[3] Some peculiar forms of the *pallium* may be seen in F at

to be the regular outer garment, though one or, possibly, two exceptions appear in the eighteen examples; the undergarment is girt up, or fastened up with a clasp, so as to be quite short on one side. In the coloured plate from C at Ph. 784, given by Weston,[1] the undergarments of the Senes are a purplish-gray and their *pallia* yellow-brown[2] (cf. the testimony of Donatus, cited on p. 96).

In the two pictures of Crito contained in P[3] (And. 796 and 904) we see that he carries a straight staff on which the knots are so prominent that it looks as if it were budded; at Ad. 718, in F, Demea has a plain stick. As Wieseler[4] has pointed out in the case of Demea, so in both pictures of Crito the stick is not the 'Krummstab' of the Senex, so often seen in reliefs[5] and wall-paintings,[5] but the 'Wanderstab' of the traveller, easily suggested to the artist of F (and, indeed, of P) by the immediate context. After examining several representations of old men on Greek vases,[6] I am

Haut. 593 (perhaps not genuine: see p. 106, n. 1), 749, 874, and at Ad. 776; in C and P at Ph. 894.

[1] Harvard Studies, 14.

[2] Cf. Bethe, 10, 20 (cited above under ADULESCENS, p. 50, n. 2).

[3] The corresponding pictures in C and O are not at my command; for F they do not exist.

[4] Denkmäler, 70 b.

[5] Wieseler, Tafeln XI u. XII; Bethe, 31.

[6] Furtwängler u. Reichhold, Griechische Vasenmalerei (München, 1900–1901).

inclined to believe that the form of the staff in the three examples cited above is not so suspicious as the fact that it occurs only in the immediate neighbourhood of a context which would remind the artist that the Senex has just returned from a journey, or from a long walk. In view of such a fact, I cannot share Bethe's sanguine [1] belief that, in the archetype, all Senes had staves.

Worthy of notice are the pictures, one in C, the other in F, immediately preceding the first scene of the Hautontimorumenos, where Chremes is striving to draw the self-tormentor from his incessant labour. The artist has apparently chosen to represent the moment when Chremes tries the weight of the *rastri* and exclaims *Hui! tam gravis hos, quaeso* (92). In C, Chremes holds a two-pronged rake, in F, a double-headed pick. Menedemus,[2] also, holds uplifted an implement which, in C, is like Chremes's rake, but, in F, is a single-headed pick. The corresponding figures in the two pictures agree remarkably well in costume, attitude, and relative position, but the two scenes differ considerably in details of setting, in spite of the fact that both represent a field.[3] The costumes

[1] Praefatio 31 ff.

[2] The commentators, generally, assume a single implement in this passage.

[3] Engelhardt, Die Illustrationen der Terenzhandschriften,

of the two men are such as Senes usually wear in the miniatures — quite unsuitable for the manual labour which Menedemus is bent on performing. Furthermore, there was a distinct tradition concerning Menedemus's dress which the artist has violated — a tradition handed down to us by Varro, when he is writing of goatskins used for clothing (De Re Rustica, 2. 11): cuius usum apud antiquos quoque Graecos fuisse apparet, quod in tragoediis senes ab hac pelle vocantur διφθερίαι, et in comoediis, qui in rustico opere morantur; ut apud Caecilium in Hyporbolimaeo habet adulescens, apud Terentium in Heautontimorumeno Senex (see RUSTICUS, pp. 135–136).

SERVUS

This rôle occurs at least once in every play of Plautus and Terence. In numerous cases we get some hint of the costume and appearance of the Servus, but only a few deliberate descriptions occur.

(1) In the Amphitruo Mercurius Deus and

---

67–68, believes that the scene took place in town before Chremes's house, as Menedemus was hurrying by to his farm in the suburbs. If this be true, the picture does not represent the stage-tradition and is an argument against the antiquity of the miniatures. For evidence, however, that the scene is in the country see Knapp, Class. Phil. 2. 17. Cf., also, the Rudens of Plautus.

Sosia Servus are quite fully described, because the plot turns in part on the fact that the god is disguised so as to be identical in appearance with the slave. Sosia's *pallium* (294) and *tunicae* (368–369) are supplemented by a *petasus* (143, 146–147, 443), because he is returning from a journey.[1] He carries a *lanterna*, too (149, 341), since he is coming home from the harbour by night. His *tonsus* and *barba*[2] are referred to in 444; the mention of the *tonsus* would seem to indicate that his *petasus* was hanging down his back.[3]

(2) The appearance of Leonida Servus is what is really given us under the pretended description of Saurea Atriensis in the As., 400–401:

> macilentis malis, rufulus, aliquantum ventriosus,
> truculentis oculis, commoda statura, tristi fronte.

(3) In Ep. 10 we again have a stout slave: *corpulentior videre atque habitior.* This slave is addressed as *adulescens* in verse 1.

(4) The appearance of Pseudolus (1218–1221) recalls that of Leonida, as quoted above under (2):

---

[1] For the traveller's costume see p. 46, n. 2.

[2] Cf. Bethe, Praefatio 53. The Terentian miniatures show some Servi with beards and moustaches.

[3] Frequent illustrations of this are seen in Greek vase-paintings. Cf. Furtwängler u. Reichhold, Griechische Vasenmalerei (München, 1900–1901).

rufus quidam, ventriosus, crassis suris, subniger, magno capite, acutis oculis, ore rubicundo, admodum magnis pedibus.

The large feet are a vital part of the description, as is shown by Ballio's words (Ps. 1220–1221): *perdidisti, ut nominavisti pedes. Pseudolus fuit ipsus.*

Thus, probably, a regular feature of the make-up of the Servus was grotesqueness.[1]

From Diomedes [2] we learn that wigs of different colours were early used to indicate the *ages* of the several Dramatis Personae: Antea galearibus, non personis utebantur, ut qualitas coloris indicium faceret aetatis cum essent aut albi aut nigri aut rufi. This passage is sometimes cited as authority for the statement that *slaves always wore red wigs.* So far as I know, we have no authority for so sweeping a statement. Pollux (Onom. IV, 149–150), writing Περὶ προσώπων κωμικῶν, speaks of the masks and wigs worn by slaves in comedy: Τὰ δὲ δούλων πρόσωπα κωμικὰ, πάππος, ἡγεμὼν, θεράπων, κάτω τριχίας, ἢ κάτω τετριχωμένος, θεράπων οὖλος, θεράπων μέσος, θεράπων τέττιξ, ἡγεμὼν ἐπίσειστος. Ὁ μὲν πάππος μόνος τῶν θεραπόντων πολιός ἐστι καὶ δηλοῖ ἀπε-

---

[1] This is well attested for the period following the introduction of masks by art, literature, and the grotesque masks which the Terentian miniatures of Servi uniformly show.

[2] Keil, Gram. Lat. 1. 489.

λεύθερον. Ὁ δὲ ἡγεμὼν θεράπων σπεῖραν ἔχει τριχῶν πυῤῥῶν, ἀνατέτακε τὰς ὀφρῦς, συνάγει τὸ ἐπισκύνιον. τοιοῦτος ἐν τοῖς δούλοις, οἷος ἐν τοῖς ἐλευθέροις πρεσβύτης ἡγεμών. Ὁ δὲ κάτω τριχίας ἢ κάτω τετριχωμένος ἀναφαλαντίας ἐστι, πυῤῥόθριξ, ἐπηρμένος τὰς ὀφρῦς. Ὁ δὲ οὖλος θεράπων, οὖλος μὲν τὰς τρίχας. εἰσὶ δὲ πυῤῥαὶ, ὥσπερ καὶ τὸ χρῶμα. καὶ ἀναφαλαντίας ἐστὶ καὶ διάστροφος τὴν ὄψιν. Ὁ δὲ θεράπων μέσος φαλακρὸς, πυῤῥός ἐστιν. Ὁ δὲ θεράπων τέττιξ μέλας, φαλακρὸς, διάστροφος τὴν ὄψιν, δύο ἢ τρία βοστρύχια μέλανα ἐπικείμενος, καὶ ὅμοια ἐν τῷ γενείῳ. Ὁ δὲ ἐπίσειστος ἡγεμὼν ἔοικε τῷ ἡγεμόνι θεράποντι, πλὴν περὶ τὰς τρίχας. It may well be that this Greek tradition of a red wig for *most* slaves was generally followed in the early Roman theatre. In Plautus, however, I find only the two[1] red-haired slaves already mentioned — Leonida (*rufulus*, As. 400) and Pseudolus (*rufus*, Ps. 1218); in Terence I note only one, Davus (*rufus*, Ph. 51). In the miniatures the wigs show varieties of style[2] as numerous as those of which Pollux writes.

As for the garments of the slave, reference is made to the *tunicae* of Sosia (Am. 368–369) and of Strobilus (Au. 647). The mention of the *pallium*

---

[1] For discussion of Philocrates Captivus see ADULESCENS, p. 45.

[2] I have no detailed information concerning the *colours* of the wigs in the miniatures.

is not very frequent (Am. 294; Au. 646; Cas. 934 [Olympio vilicus]; Ep. 1, 194 [*palliolum* [1]] Ps. 1275, 1279, 1281; Ph. 844, 863). Characteristic is the manner of wearing the *pallium*, which I shall discuss in connection with the miniatures of Servi (see pp. 106–108).

In the Trinummus (720) the *soccus* seems to be Stasimus's regular shoe. He is the only slave who is mentioned as having a *condalium* (Tri. 1014, 1022).

From the nature of the plots the Servi often carry money and so have a *crumina* (As. 590, 653 [Leonida Atriensis]; Ep. 360; Per. 265, 317), a *marsuppium* (carried by Messenio Servus, Men. 265, 272, 384–386), a *mellina* (Ep. 23). Wholly dependent upon the individual plot, and, therefore, not an essential part of the slave-costume *per se* are many articles which slaves carry in special cases — *obsonium, litterae, fustes, vasa, tabellae, ferramenta,* etc.

### TESTIMONY OF THE MINIATURES

I have examined about one hundred and fifty miniatures of Servi, approximately two-fifths of that number being from F, one-third from P, and the remaining four-fifteenths from C and O (with

---

[1] Apud Gellium 4. 17. 4, however, we have the reading *pallium.*

a slight preponderance in favour of C). The results show a very general uniformity in the stock-costume and illustrate well Donatus's statement (De Com. VIII, 6): servi comici amictu exiguo teguntur paupertatis antiquae gratia vel quo expeditiores agant.[1]

The tunic varies in length, sometimes reaching nearly to the ankle, sometimes girt as high as the knee, or, as in O, even higher. Its sleeves are generally close [2] and reach regularly to the wrist.[3]

---

[1] In Ru. 573–575 Charmides begs Sceparnio to give him *vestimenti aliquid aridi.* Sceparnio replies (576–577):

> Tegillum e(c)cillud, mihi unum id aret: id si vis, dabo.
> Eodem amictus, eodem tectus esse soleo, si pluit.

We must, perhaps, discount these words, for (1) Sceparnio is purposely ungracious to Charmides as the comrade of Labrax the Leno, and (2) he is slave of a poor master (Ru., pr. 33–38).

[2] In F, three cases of Servi show, in addition to the long, close sleeve here mentioned, a wide oversleeve reaching almost to the elbow. At Eun. 923 and 1031 this flowing sleeve is seen on the right arm of Parmeno Servus; at Haut. 593 it appears on the left arm (probably, also, on the right arm) of Syrus Servus, his back being turned to the audience. For the validity of this picture see p. 106, n. 1.

[3] The long tunic sleeve is not what we should expect in the case of a Servus (Simia disguised as a Cacula has a *manuleata tunica* (Ps. 738), but he is said to look like a *foreigner* (Ps. 964)). Cf. Pollux, Onom. IV, 119, VII, 47 χιτὼν δὲ ὁ μὲν ἀμφιμάσχαλος ἐλευθέρων σχῆμα, ὁ δὲ ἑτερομάσχαλος οἰκετῶν; Hesychius (a late authority), cited by Baumeister, *s.v. Lustspiel*, 825 B, n. 31 ἑτερομάσχαλος· χιτὼν δουλικὸς ἐργατικός· ἀπο (τοῦ) τὴν ἑτέραν μασχάλην ἔχειν ἐρραμένην. Wieseler, how-

When the hands are not employed in gesticulation or in some other way, there regularly hangs down in front, from the left[1] shoulder, a scarf which the Servus grasps with his left hand. Not infrequently the scarf goes around the neck behind and is grasped by both hands in front (And. 796, 957, in P); or, hanging from the left shoulder in front, it passes around the shoulder, winds around the right arm and hangs from it (And. 338, in P). By far the greatest variety in the arrangement of this scarf is shown by the miniatures of P, but it is impossible to draw any inference from that fact, since the corresponding scenes in other MSS. are not available for comparison.

---

ever, declares (Denkmäler, 76 a) that, not only in the Terentian miniatures, but even on other representations of stage-scenes, the right arm of the slave is seldom bare. See also Baumeister, Denkmäler, under *Chiton*, and *Lustspiel*, 825 A, and Smith, Dictionary of Greek and Roman Antiquities[3], under *Tunica*. For the bearing of this long tunic sleeve on the date of the miniatures see p. 49, n. 2.

[1] Exceptional is Syrus Servus (Haut. 593, in F), whose scarf hangs from his *right* shoulder and is grasped by his *right* hand, his back being towards the audience. Engelhardt (Die Illustrationen der Terenzhandschriften, 10) calls attention to the fact that this picture is not found in C and P and that the position of Syrus, who stands with his back directly to the spectators and with his head turned over his shoulder, is quite unique. For this and other reasons Engelhardt believes that the picture may have originated with the artist of F, who had to insert something at this point, because in his text a new scene began here.

It is, apparently, this scarf which Pollux mentions in Onomasticon (IV, 119): τῇ δὲ τῶν δούλων ἐξωμίδι καὶ ἱματίδιόν τι προσκεῖται λευκόν, ὃ ἐγκόμβωμα λέγεται, ἢ ἐπίῤῥημα. But, even without the aid of this passage, it is probable that many persons, examining the miniatures, have conjectured that the scarf was a conventionalized form of the *pallium collectum*[1] of the *servus currens*. So natural a conjecture is rendered especially easy by certain miniatures which show, besides this scarf, traces of the lower edge of a *pallium* running diagonally across the tunic skirt (*e.g.*, And. 481, P; Haut. 512, 593, F; Ph. 606, F). Apparently somewhat contradictory to this theory are the miniatures of Geta Servus in C and P at Ph. 841, for, though Geta is clearly referring to the *pallium collectum* in 844–845,[2] the miniatures of both C and

---

[1] Cf. Cap. 778–779:

> eodem pacto ut comici servi solent,
> coniciam in collum pallium, primo ex med hanc rem ut audiat;

Cap. 789; Ep. 194:

> age nunciam orna te, Epidice, et palliolum in collum conice
> itaque adsimulato quasi per urbem totam hominem quaesiveris.

Ph. 844–845; etc. For discussion see Wieseler, Denkmäler, 73–75.

[2] sed ego nunc mihi cesso, qui non umerum hunc onero *pallio*
atque hominem propero invenire, ut haec quae contigerint sciat.

P show the *pallium* piled high on his back; however, in C Geta's left hand grasps a short end of the *pallium* on the left shoulder, and in P this end amounts to quite a long scarf. The picture in F is lacking at this point, but that in O shows no *pallium* on the slave's back, while the scarf at the left is in more thoroughly conventionalized form than usual, having little or no connection with Geta's tunic.

It is not always possible to see the means by which the tunic is girded, but it is often done by means of a string or a scarf. The point of fastening varies, being at the side or sides, or at the back or front. In O there are clear cases of a *fibula* in place of a string or scarf (see Ph. 713, 728, in O).

### VIRGO

This rôle is found once in the Aulularia, Curculio, Epidicus, Persa, Hautontimorumenos, and Adelphoe, but we have very little information about the various Virgines.

Planesium of the Curculio is *lepida* (167), *nimis lepida* (said sarcastically), *bella* (521). She probably had large, dark eyes, for the angry Palinurus says spitefully (190–192):

> quid ais, propudium?
> tun etiam *cum noctuinis oculis* 'odium' me vocas,
> ebriola persolla, nugae?

She wears an *anulus*, by which she proves to her brother her identity.

Telestis is described in the following words (Ep. 623):

usque ab unguiculo ad capillum summumst festivissuma.

Lucris Virgo is *forma lepida et liberali* (Per. 130). Her general appearance in her disguise as a *peregrina* is quite fully described (130, 157–158, 335, 521, 546–548, 564), but we find mention of only one of the articles that she wears — the *crepidula* (464).

Antiphila Virgo (Mulier) passes as an attendant of Bacchis Meretrix, *servolae habitum gerens* (Haut. Per. 7–8). Sostrata Matrona refers to her as *quam Bacchis secum adduxit adulescentulam* (654).

### TESTIMONY OF THE MINIATURES

I have examined three or four pictures of the Virgo.

(1) In P at Eun. 454 the figures bear two sets of names, one above, the other below, the picture. The second from the end, beginning at the right, is designated as *Virgo* above and as *Pythias Ancilla* below. She is doubtless the Ethiopian girl who is being led as a present to Thais. Her costume, except for the absence of every trace of a mantle, is hardly distinguishable

from that of an Ancilla, though the long line extending down the left side of her gown is unusual.

(2) At Haut. 381, in P, we find Antiphila Virgo, designated in the picture, however, as *Antiphila Mulier.* The details of her costume are not clear because she is being embraced by Clinia Adulescens. She shows the long undergarment and traces of a *pallium;* probably she has the double set of sleeves so often found in the miniatures. Her hair is arranged low in her neck; the high knot or ornament on top of her head is askew.

(3) At Haut. 381, in F, the designation is merely *Antiphila.* Her costume is essentially the same as in P at the same point, save that her mantle is drawn over her head and carefully arranged in folds. The drawing of the outer sleeve implies an impossible arrangement of the mantle.

(4) Possibly we should include among the miniatures of the Virgo the picture of a woman found at Eun. 232, in P; she must be Pamphila (Virgo? cf. 229, 440), whom Gnatho is leading to Thais as a present from Thraso Miles. The picture shows a long undergarment, probably the two sets of sleeves, and traces of a *pallium.* Her hair is rather elaborately dressed low in her neck, and she wears an ornamented head-band.

# CHAPTER V

## UNUSUAL RÔLES

### ADVOCATUS

*Advocati* appear in the Poenulus and the Phormio.

(1) In the Poenulus (531, 723–727, 765–767) the Advocati are summoned by Agorastocles Adulescens, to serve as witnesses in a suit which he intends to bring against a dishonest Leno (800–807). The details of their costumes are in no way indicated, but some idea of their appearance may be gained from what is told of their origin and of certain physical peculiarities. The Advocati are not *senes*,[1] for Agorastocles, in his eager haste, had deliberately avoided summoning certain friends of his who were old (508–509); but old men might as well have been summoned, for these Advocati are gouty (532) and bow-legged (510: see, however, Ussing's note), and seem to the impatient Adulescens to be coming at less than a snail's pace (506–507, 512–513, 532). They are evidently *libertini* (519–523), a fact of which

[1] Poe. 783 does not necessarily imply that they are old.

Agorastocles takes advantage when he suggests that their slow gait is due to their having had to walk in fetters (513–514); later they refer to themselves as *Aetoli cives* (621)[1]. They admit that to a rich youth like Agorastocles they must seem *plebeii et pauperes* (515, 536). They are said by Milphio Servus to frequent the comitium even more than the praetor does (584–587), to be, in fact, men who live by lawsuits.

(2) Concerning Terence's Advocati the text of the Phormio gives us no information, but the miniatures are particularly interesting. These occur at the beginning of the third and fourth scenes of Act II (348, 441). In all four MSS. (C, P, F, O) at verse 348 the three Advocati appear in the same order, and the attitude of each is essentially the same in the four representations; at 441 the order is changed, but the change occurs in all the MSS. (C, P, F: O is lacking).

At 348 in C Hegio wears an undergarment reaching midway between the knees and the ankles, and a dark mantle fastened, *chlamys*-like, on the right shoulder and reaching to the bottom of the undergarment on the left side. The one visible sleeve of the undergarment seems to be long and close. The face is youthful. There are two

---

[1] The scene is laid in Calydon in Aetolia (pr. 94).

dark patches on the undergarment, one over each knee; this is also true of Hegio in C at 441,[1] where his costume is essentially the same, but the face is perhaps older. In P, Hegio's costume is essentially the same (this MS. is not coloured), but no patches occur on the undergarment, nor, indeed, on any but the two in C, mentioned above. In both representations in P he holds something (a document?) in his left hand. In F, Hegio's outer garment is less *chlamys*-like at 348; at 441 it is a mantle pinned in front. In both places a long, close sleeve from an undergarment appears on the right arm. It is difficult to see how the effect of the loose, flowing oversleeve suggested by both of these drawings could actually have resulted from the garments worn.[2] In O, at 348, Hegio wears a mantle that fastens, *chlamys*-like, on the right shoulder, as in C and P: this mantle is decorated with the border that is characteristic of garments in O (cf. pp. 60, 71).

Cratinus wears an undergarment with short, flowing sleeves, beneath which long, close sleeves are seen in both pictures in C, P, and F. His overgarment is a *pallium* in all six cases; in C it is darker than the undergarment. In all six

---

[1] Cf. also Thraso Miles, Eun. 391 and 454 (P).

[2] In these two miniatures Weston's drawings are unusually inferior to Bethe's photographic reproductions.

cases he carries an open book in his left hand. O is lacking at 441, but at 348 in O Cratinus wears a long-sleeved undergarment reaching to the right ankle, but caught up almost to the knee, and his outer garment is arranged like a *chlamys*. In all seven representations of him he has a big-mouthed mask. He is distinctly older than the other Advocati.

Crito wears a straight, scant, long-sleeved undergarment in C at 348, and his dark mantle is fastened *chlamys*-like on the right shoulder; at 441 the folds of the undergarment and the loose, flowing oversleeve effect are troublesome. In P at 348 Crito is blurred and hardly visible, but at 441 he is young, wears a *chlamys* and short undergarment, and has two sets of sleeves beneath his *chlamys*. In F he is essentially the same as in C. The single representation of Crito in O shows a *chlamys*-like outer garment with border, while the roll which Crito carries at 348 [1] in C and F (P is blurred and partly invisible) is so modified in O as to be unrecognizable.

The youthful appearance of Hegio and Crito as contrasted with that of Cratinus is noticeable throughout; somewhat less marked is the contrast between their dress and that of Cratinus. It is,

---

[1] None of the MSS. shows this roll at 441.

however, worthy of notice that the main inconsistency is in O, where alone the *chlamys*-like garment is given to Cratinus.

### CACULA

The Cacula[1] as a Dramatis Persona appears only in the Pseudolus. Soldiers are, however, attended by *servi* in other plays.

(1) Such a *servus* is evidently addressed in Ep. 433.

(2) In the Miles, Palestrio is a slave of Pyrgopolinices Miles, and other slaves seem to be carrying out Philocomasium's baggage at the direction of the Miles and his servant (1388 ff.); but we get no information about the costume of these *servi* — perhaps they were ordinary house-slaves, not particularly soldier's slaves.

(3) In the Eunuchus Thraso Miles directs his *servi* in a mock siege on the house of a *meretrix*. One carries a crowbar (Eun. 774), another a sponge (777–779). For description of the pertinent miniatures see, under Stock-Rôles, LORARIUS, p. 70.

The Cacula of the Pseudolus is the slave (594,

---

[1] *Cacula* servus militis. Plautus "video caculam militarem." Dicitur autem a Graeco κᾶλον, quod fustibus clavisque ligneis ad tutelam dominorum armari soliti sunt. So Festus, p. 32 (Thewrewk de Ponor).

718, 1150, 1152, 1210; cf. 1091) of a Macedonian soldier (616, 1090, 1152, 1210); he is young[1] (615, 1137, 1141; cf. 978). He is sent by his master to pay to the Leno the balance due on a girl whom the Miles loves. He looks like a stranger (foreigner?), as is indicated perhaps by *ignobilis* (592); moreover, Simia Sycophanta, who counterfeits Harpax Cacula, is described as *peregrina facie* and *ignobilis* (964). He wears a *chlamys* (1101, 1139, 1143, 1184) and a *petasus* (1186) and carries a *machaera* (593, 1185). In verse 735, where Pseudolus proposes to disguise Simia Sycophanta as Harpax, he says that he needs for the purpose a *chlamys*, a *machaera*, and a *petasus*, and he adds in 738 *Manuleatam tunicam habere hominem addecet*, which reminds us of the tunic of another *peregrinus*, Hanno Poenus (see under Unusual Rôles, POENUS, p. 134). Harpax brings a *symbolus* and money, and may well be wearing a *crumina* (598, 718, etc., etc.). Perhaps there is in his bearing something that suggests the braggart soldier, for Simia, who counterfeits Harpax, bears himself *magnifice* (911), and Simia says in 917–918:

> Quippe ego te ni contemnam,
> stratioticus homo qui cluear?

---

[1] Lorenz's objection to *adulescens* as applied to a *cacula* seems to me unjustifiable. See his note on Mo. 653.

There is nothing in 603 to indicate that the Cacula's costume is peculiar, for Pseudolus knows about the Miles (370–377) and has overheard 596–599.

Interesting and pertinent to the discussion of this rôle are the words of Stasimus Servus (Tri. 719–727), whose young master insists upon giving up his farm that his sister may not be obliged to go undowered to a husband:

quid ego nunc agam
nisi uti sarcinam constringam et clipeum ad dorsum accommodem,
fulmentas iubeam suppingi soccis? non sisti potest.
Video caculam militarem me futurum ⟨h⟩aud longius.
†At aliquem ad regem in saginam erus sese coniecit meus,
credo ad summos bellatores acrem — fugitorem fore,
et capturum spolia ibi — illum qui ero advorsus venerit.
Egomet autem quom extemplo arcum et pharetram et sagittas sumpsero,
Cassidem in caput, — dormibo placide in tabernaculo.
Ad forum ibo: nudius sextus quoi talentum mutuom
dedi reposcam, ut habeam mecum quod feram viaticum.

## CAPTIVUS

In the Captivi of Plautus Philocrates and Tyndarus are captives in a strange land, as they suppose; but Philocrates is an Elean Adulescens and Tyndarus, his *servus*, is the lost son of Hegio Senex, into whose hands both youths have fallen. For the purposes of the plot they have changed names and clothing (pr. 37, 39). Their only distinctive mark as Captivi is that they are in chains (*cum catenis sumus,*[1] 203). That they are bound is also shown by the remarks concerning them addressed to the slaves (354–355). Tyndarus wore a *collare* at first (357); in 659, after the escape of his comrade, the Lorarii are bidden to put *manicae* on him and bind his hands firmly (667). In 997 he comes in from his work in the stone-quarries, fettered (997) and carrying a pickax or crowbar (1004); he is wearing *compedes* (1025–1027).

### CHORAGUS

A Choragus appears as a Dramatis Persona in the Curculio. Nothing is suggested concerning his costume or make-up. He expresses his anxiety for his *ornamenta* which have fallen into the hands of the tricky Parasitus, Curculio.

### DANISTA

Only twice in all of Plautus and not once in Terence do we find the rôle of Danista, a fact which is rather surprising in view of the nature

---

[1] Morris emends pr. 2 to *Iuncti* astant.

of the conventional New Comedy plot (the Trapezita occurs only once, in the Curculio).

In Ep. 620 the Danista is referred to as *ille gravastellus;* in 631–632 he holds out his *crumina* for Stratippocles to put in the money that is due.

In Mo. 653 the Danista, Mysargyrides, is addressed as *adulescens.* This strikes us as unsuitable, in view of the epithet just assigned to the Danista of the Epidicus and, also, in view of the traits commonly associated with the money-lender in literature. Lorenz, in his note on the passage, cites other uses of *adulescens* which he considers surprising and which I have mentioned under the individual rôles in question.[1]

### DI

Besides Lar Familiaris (Au.), Auxilium Deus (Ci.), and Arcturus (Ru.), who have already been treated under PROLOGUS (pp. 39–40), Plautus introduces as Dramatis Personae in his unique Amphitruo two more important personages, the gods Mercurius and Iuppiter. The former serves as Prologus; but, even when speaking the prologue, he is already dressed for his rôle in the play (pr. 117–119, 121–123), the rôle of a Servus (*q.v.*).

Since the plot turns on the perfect disguise of these gods, the one as Amphitruo Dux, the other

---

[1] See pp. 87, 116 n. 1, 137.

as Sosia Servus, their costumes must have borne a somewhat accurate resemblance to those of the mortals whom they were counterfeiting. Somewhat accurate, I say, for certain details, such as the lantern of Sosia (pr. 149, 341, 406), may have varied in the corresponding costumes. So strong was the resemblance between the genuine and the counterfeit in each case that none of the other Dramatis Personae detected the fraud, and even the counterfeited persons were completely mystified (265–266, 441–446, 601, 864–866; Acts IV and V; cf. Arg. I. 1. 4–5, 7, II. 1–2, 4–8; pr. 121–124, 129, 134–135, 141 and the references in the next paragraph to the prologue).

For the convenience of the audience a single mark of distinction was allowed in the case of each pair: Mercury's costume differed from Sosia's in *pennulae* worn *in petaso* (pr. 143) and Iuppiter's from Amphitruo's in a *torulus aureus* worn *sub petaso* (pr. 144–145). By a stage-convention both of these marks were invisible to the other players (pr. 146–147). The doubtful Plautine origin of the Amphitruo Prologue casts discredit on this evidence, but some such device would certainly have been natural, if not necessary.[1]

---

[1] Cf. the device used by Messrs. Robson and Crane when they played the Dromios in the Comedy of Errors; one wore a patch on one side of his face, the other on the other.

Even a casual reader must ask himself in what guise Iuppiter appeared in the second scene of the last act (1131–1143). Palmer (Am. Int., p. xiv) assumes that the god "appears in *his proper form* amid peals of thunder."[1] Verses 1130–1131 lend colour to such an assumption, for Iuppiter at once hastens to reassure Amphitruo, who seems more terrified than mere thunder and lightning might warrant. In such a case, one would like to know what was considered the god's "proper form" in the Roman theatre of Plautus's time. If we may judge from the representations of the god in art, a very slight change from his former appearance would have been sufficient; in Greek vase-painting the common attributes of Zeus are a crown, sceptre, throne, and thunderbolt. It would obviously have been desirable for Iuppiter to keep as nearly as possible to his resemblance to Amphitruo, for thus the latter would have been able to recognize him (1) as the cause of all the confusion in Act IV, and (2) as the personage who had been able to deceive the innocent Alcumena. His divine nature could have been sufficiently attested by the mighty thunder which heralded his approach (1130) and by a blinding light (cf. Bromia's soliloquy in 1053–1070). We must

[1] The italics are my own.

remember that Amphitruo has been prepared for some such miraculous dénouement by Bromia's account of the birth of the twins, of the strange behaviour of one of them, and of the voice of Iuppiter acknowledging this child as his son (1053–1124).

The *scipio* which Iuppiter carries at verse 520 would probably not suggest the god's sceptre, but was merely part of his disguise as Amphitruo, who might have carried a staff (1) as *Dux*, a position of dignity and honour, or (2) as *Senex* (1072: see SENEX, p. 96), or (3) as one just returned from a journey (see p. 98).

For an interesting vase-painting showing Zeus and Hermes before the window of Alcmene see Wieseler, Denkmäler, IX, 11; the scene is possibly from the Amphitruo of Rhinthon.

### DUX

Amphitruo Dux is leader of an expedition sent out from Thebes against the Teleboae. He arrives home victorious at the opening of the play.

Even if the prologue of the Amphitruo is not Plautine, the inference from verses 144–147 that Amphitruo wears a *petasus* is probably safe enough, since it is the regular hat of travellers (p. 46, n. 2). From 854 we conclude that he has *pedisequi*, who probably entered with him at 654. In 1072 he is referred to as a *senex*,[1] for whose traditional make-up see SENEX (pp. 92–100). That a *scipio* would not have been unfitting is further shown by the fact that one was carried by Iuppiter, who so successfully counterfeited him.

### EUNUCHUS

The real Eunuchus of Terence's play is described as *decrepitus* (231) and is referred to as *illum . . . inhonestum hominem, . . . senem mulierem* (356–357). Chaerea, who counterfeits him, is young and fair to look upon. It is not necessary to make himself up to look like the real Eunuchus, for Thais and her household have never seen the latter. So, when Dorus, the genuine Eunuchus, is presented to them, Pythias Ancilla exclaims (680–682):

> Au,
> ne comparandus quidem hic ad illumst[2]: ille erat
> honesta facie ac liberali.

To which Phaedria replies (682–684):

> Ita visus est
> dudum, quia varia veste exornatus fuit;
> nunc tibi videtur foedus, quia illam non habet.

---

[1] See p. 93, n. 1.

[2] *Illum* denotes the counterfeit Eunuchus.

In 688–689 Pythias again maintains that this is not the youth who was brought to them:

> hic est vietus vetus veternosus senex,
> colore mustelino.[1]

Later, when Pythias's accusations are being confirmed by the independent statements of the real Eunuchus, Phaedria himself exclaims in 704 ff.,

> Age nunc, beluae
> credis huic quod dicat?

The *varia vestis* of the real Eunuchus must have been somewhat striking, for Antipho, seeing Chaerea disguised in it, exclaims (558 ff.):

> Chaerea, quid est quod sic gestis? quidve hic vestitus sibi quaerit?

and Phaedria, who has unexpectedly returned from the country and heard what has happened at Thais's home, finding Dorus Eunuchus, whom he supposes to be the guilty man, comments at once (670) on his change of dress and interprets it as meaning that the Eunuchus is preparing to flee (673).

I have had access to five illustrations which show the costume of the Eunuchus — the pictures from P at 454 and 539, and from F at 539, 668, and 840.

---

[1] Proof of Dorus's foreign origin?

The first is unsatisfactory on account of an evident confusion of rôles. Engelhardt[1] declares that the figure designated 'Par' in P is 'Chaerea' in C; since the costume of 'Par' in P is impossible for a slave and very suitable for the Eunuchus, we may assume an error on the part of the illustrator of P and accept 'Par' as the disguised Chaerea. The probable pseudo-Eunuchus in P, then, wears a long-sleeved undergarment, girt above the knees, a mantle fastened squarely in front on the chest and thrown back over both shoulders and, most characteristic of all, a Phrygian cap, which marks his Oriental origin. In both illustrations at verse 539 Chaerea's costume corresponds almost exactly to that of the genuine Eunuchus at 454, P; the principal difference lies in the addition of the familiar short, flowing, oversleeve on the left arm in P and on both arms in F.

The illustration from F at 668 is unsatisfactory, for, where it should represent an ugly, decrepit *senex*, we find (unless we suppose a rather doubtful confusion of names in this picture) a particularly youthful face and figure designated 'Eunuc ?'. The costume answers fairly well to that of an Adulescens. It looks as if the original illustrator, not familiar with the plot, had suited the face

---

[1] Die Illustrationen der Terenzhandschriften, 65.

and figure to the youthful costume which the old Eunuchus had received in exchange for his own from Chaerea Adulescens. At 840 in F we are supposed to find Chaerea disguised as the Eunuchus. The mantle is entirely lacking; the short undergarment is regular and two sets of sleeves are visible, as at verse 539, in F.

### FIDICINA

In the Epidicus Fidicinae appear. They seem to belong to the class known as *meretrices*. Epidicus relates how the one beloved by Stratippocles went to meet him on his return from Thebes (Ep. 212–221) and was attended by four *tibicinae* (218); she was, furthermore, most elaborately bedecked and bejewelled (222 ff.). When the hired Fidicina is brought to his house, Periphanes gives careful directions to keep her away from his (supposed) daughter, for (403)

> divortunt mores virgini longe ac lupae,

a sentiment applauded by his friend Apoecides, who says (404–405):

> docte et sapienter dicis. num ⟨quam⟩ nimis potest
> pudicitiam quisquam suae servare filiae.

This Fidicina has been hired under false pretences (411–418); she brings her *fides* with her (411–418, 500), for, later in the play, when Epidicus's trick is discovered and Periphanes angrily bids the Fidicina be off, she says *Fides non reddis?* (514–516). Both Fidicinae seem to have been freedwomen (496–498, 505). Epidicus speaks of Acropolistis as having been an *ancilla* (131). The bearing of both was probably pert and free (399–404, 413, 577–578).

### GUBERNATOR

The Gubernator appears only once — in the Amphitruo of Plautus. He is Blepharo,[1] the pilot of the ship in which Amphitruo returned home from his expedition against the Teleboae (949–951). He is summoned to arbitrate between the troubled Amphitruo and his counterfeit, Iuppiter (1035–1040).

From the play we get no information about his costume, but an excellent description of the dress of a *gubernator* is given in the Miles (1177–1184), where the disguise of Pleusicles is planned:

facito ut⟨i⟩ venias *ornatu* huc ad nos *nauclerico.*
*causiam* habeas *ferrugineam* et *scutulam ob oculos laneam:*
*palliolum* habeas *ferrugineum,* nam is colos thalassicust:
*id conexum in umero laevo,* exfafillato bracchio

[1] "The man who keeps a good look-out ahead" (cf. βλέπειν): see Palmer's note on Amphitruo, Arg. II, 8. Cf. Schmidt, Griechische Personennamen bei Plautus, Hermes 37, 357.

* * * * * * *

atque apud hunc senem omnia haec sunt: nam is piscatores[1] habet.

For further references to some of the same particulars of Pleusicles's disguise, see Mi. 1282, 1286, 1306–1309, 1430.

### MEDICUS

The Medicus appears among the Dramatis Personae of a single play, the Menaechmi. We find no reference to his costume, though his character and mannerisms are well delineated. To the father-in-law of Menaechmus II the Medicus is *odiosus* (884); he takes his time in answering the summons of the old man, and is full of boasts about his own skill (882–888). Verses 899–965 contain the picture of this character.

### MERCATOR

There are two plays from which we might expect information regarding this rôle — the Asinaria and the Mercator.

In the former, some Arcadian asses having been sold to a Mercator from Pella (As. 333–337), a youth arrives bringing money in payment, intended for Demaenetus's steward, Saurea. This

---

[1] In view of the implied similarity between the costume of a *piscator* and a *gubernator* see PISCATOR, pp. 131–132.

Adulescens (337) seems to be the person who is styled in the scene-headings and in the list of Dramatis Personae 'Mercator Chlamydatus.' He refers to himself as a *peregrinus* (464) [1] and he has just arrived after a journey; so the *chlamys* seems natural. He probably had some sort of purse — perhaps a *crumina* [2] for the twenty minae which he brought (435–473, 487, 494, 503).

In the Mercator, Charinus Adulescens has just returned from a long trading-journey; he tells us that he is on his way from the ship in the harbour (109), but nothing is indicated concerning his costume.[3] Later in the play, maddened by the loss of his *amica,* he prepares to go on an expedition in search of her (851–863). For the garb which he there proposes to assume see MILES, pp. 79–80.

## OBSTETRIX

This rôle is found only in the Andria. The play itself suggests nothing concerning the costume of Lesbia Obstetrix, but two pictures of her occur in P, one at verse 459, the other at 481. There is a confusion of names in the former illustration, but in the latter the dress of Lesbia is not to be distinguished from that of other

[1] See p. 83, n. 1. [2] Cf. Tru. 954–956. [3] See p. 46, n. 2.

women. She wears a long tunic, with short, flowing sleeve, and a mantle that follows the usual lines of a *pallium*. This, too, is the costume of the figure at verse 459 who probably ought to be identified with Lesbia.

### PAEDAGOGUS

In the Bacchides we find Lydus Servus acting as the *paedagogus* of Pistoclerus Adulescens (see especially 138, 142, 148, 152 ff., 368–384). Lydus is the *magister* (148, 152, 404 ff., 440–448) and Pistoclerus the *discipulus* (467, 484). The relation existing between the two is clear, but nothing is said concerning the costume of the *paedagogus*.

As is the case in this play, the Greek *paedagogus* was usually a slave. It was the business of such a slave to attend his young master in public places, carrying to school and to the palaestra the boy's books, writing-materials, strigil, and oil-flask. Baumeister[1] says that in sculptures representing mythological subjects the *paedagogus* is often portrayed as a barbarian in features and costume, wearing a short *chiton* with sleeves, a rough mantle and high boots, and carrying in his hand a knotty stick (cf. the *paedagogus* in the

[1] Denkmäler, 2. 1125 ff.

celebrated Niobe group[1] and the *paedagogus* of Medea's children[2]). In real life, however, from the fifth century on, the *paedagogus* was not distinguishable as a *foreign* slave. He was generally an old man who wore a *himation* or a *chiton* (cf. vase-paintings of the period).

Of course it must have been this latter type of *paedagogus* who appeared in *fabulae palliatae,* and in the case of Lydus there was probably nothing to distinguish his dress from that of any elderly slave attending his master.

## PISCATOR

The only play in which a Piscator appears as a Dramatis Persona is the Rudens, though in the Stichus Pinacium Puer, who had been sent to the harbour to watch incoming ships in hope of his master's arrival, seems to have intended to while away his time there fishing, for on his return he carries a *harundo,* a *sportula,* and a *hamulus piscarius* (St. 289, 319–321), and Gelasimus asks him, *Iam tu piscator factu's?* (St. 317).[3]

In the Rudens the introduction of a group of Piscatores (Act II, 1) must have been rather effective in furnishing local colour and in preparing the way for Gripus, on whose catch of the *vidulus* (Ru.

[1] See Baumeister, Denkmäler, under *Scopas,* Abb. 1750.
[2] See Mon. d. Inst. XI, 31, no. 11.
[3] See p. 91.

908–913) the plot turns. These fishermen were poor creatures, living from hand to mouth and shabbily dressed[1] (295–305). They carried *hami* and *harundines* (294). Quintilian (11. 3. 112) groups *piscatores* with *servi*, *ancillae*, and *parasiti*, as follows: Itaque in fabulis iuvenum, senum, militum, matronarum gravior ingressus est: servi, ancillae, parasiti, piscatores citatius moventur.

Gripus Piscator is a *slave* (Ru. 918, 928–930, etc.) who has chanced to bring up in his net (942–943, 1020, etc.) a *vidulus* (987, etc., etc.) containing, among other things, the *cistella caudea* (1109–1110, 1142) in which are the *crepundia* (1081–1082, 1154–1171)[2] of the shipwrecked Palaestra. To the *vidulus* is attached the *rudens* (938–939, 1015, 1031) from which the play takes its name. In verses 1299–1302 Gripus is polishing a rusty spit (*veru*).

### POENA

In the Poenulus we are told that Giddenis Nutrix, with her two charges, the daughters of Hanno Poenus, was sold to a *leno*. She may not

---

[1] The following note from Sonnenschein's Ru., Act II, 1 (edit. minor), is plausible: "They are dressed in the ordinary costume of peasants on the stage — a white sleeveless *chiton* (ἐξωμίς), perhaps with a covering of skins (διφθέραι) — and carry their fishing apparatus on their backs."

[2] For the various articles comprising the *crepundia* of Palaestra see verses 1154–1171.

have been of Carthaginian blood, but the inference that she was is at least tempting. Her *statura haud magna* (1112) reminds us of Hanno Poenus (see p. 134) *hallex viri* (1310), and her dusky skin (1112) and black eyes (1113) suggest African origin; cf. 1111–1114:

Sed earum nutrix *qua* sit *facie*, mi expedi:
(Mi.) Statura haud magna, corpore aquilost — (Ha.) Ipsa east.
(Mi.) Specie *venusta, ore* atque *oculis pernigris.*
(Ha.) Formam quidem hercle verbis depinxti probe.

For the ordinary NUTRIX see pp. 84–85.

### POENUS (HANNO)

Hanno, the Carthaginian, comes to Calydon in Aetolia to seek his lost daughters, who, as appears in the sequel, have fallen into the hands of Lycus Leno. Hanno is referred to in 1031 as *peregrinus* and *advena* and in the post-Plautine prologue as a *senex* (83).

Hanno is represented in this prologue as knowing "all languages" (112–113). He enters at verse 930, speaking some unintelligible tongue, presumably that of a Poenus, but he soon falls into the vernacular of his audience and explains to them his mission. After the entrance (961) of Agorastocles and his slave, Milphio, he talks for a time in the Punic tongue, which the rascally *servus* pretends to interpret correctly to his young master. At last the angry foreigner breaks into Latin and explains the situation for himself.

The costume of the Poenus is unusual. He wears no *pallium* (976), but his long tunics (1298) seem to be voluminous (975,[1] 1121) and to be bound by no girdle (1008, 1303 [2]); hence Antamoenides's contemptuous words, *genus hoc mulierosumst* (1303). Verse 977 (*facies quidem edepol Punicast: guggast homo*) is a questionable line. Hanno is very short, a *hallex viri* (1310); the following lines are not clear, except as they suggest that the Carthaginian's breath smells of leeks and garlic.

Hanno is attended by aged slaves,[3] who carry his baggage and wear rings in their ears (978–981). He brings a *tessera hospitalis* (958, 1047–1052).

### RUSTICUS

Among the Dramatis Personae of the Truculentus we find a character styled Strabax Adule-

---

[1] Has he long tunic sleeves, suggesting the wings of a bird? This would be *mulierosum*. Ussing thinks not; see his note on 973.

[2] Cf. Ussing's note on *tunicis demissiciis*, 1303: "usque ad talos demissis, quales mulieres gestabant et viri effeminati"; cf. Hor. Serm. 1. 2. 25; Cic. Cat. 2. 10. 22 manicatis et talaribus tunicis; Verr. 5. 13. 31 cum iste cum pallio purpureo talarique tunica versaretur in conviviis muliebribus.

[3] They are probably badly bent over.

scens Rusticus. He is the son of a man who has a house in town and a farm in the country, but the atmosphere of the country surrounds both Strabax and his father's slave, Stratulax. The slave is a sour, ill-tempered fellow (251–254, 265, 308–317, 673) whose language and conversation smack of the farm (268 ff., 688 ff.), but we hear nothing of his costume.

Strabax Adulescens Rusticus comes to town from the farm, wearing about his neck a *crumina* (655, 956), containing the money paid to his father by a sheep-buyer. His generally countrified appearance and bearing are first suggested by his reference to his rivals for Phronesium's favour as *urbanos istos mundulos amasios* (658). In 922 ff. his sensitiveness over his stupid bearing again appears. In 930 his rival, the Miles, says to Phronesium,

> Qui, malum, bella aut faceta's, quae ames *homine⟨m⟩ isti modi?*

and again in 933,

> Huncine hominem te amplexari tam *horridum ac ta⟨m⟩ squalidum?*

Pollux, writing of costumes in comedy (Onom. IV, 119), says πήρα, βακτηρία, διφθέρα ἐπὶ τῶν ἀγροίκων. A little further on (120) he remarks τοῖς δὲ παρασίτοις πρόσεστι καὶ στλεγγὶς καὶ λήκυθος, ὡς τοῖς ἀγροίκοις λαγωβόλον. Interesting in connection with the former passage is the one already cited from Varro (De Re Rustica, 2. 11) under SENEX, p. 100. Valuable, too, is the following sentence from Pollux's chapter on the Masks of the New Comedy (Onom. IV, 147): τῷ δὲ ἀγροίκῳ τὸ μὲν χρῶμα μελαίνεται, τὰ δὲ χείλη πλατέα, καὶ ἡ ῥὶς σιμὴ καὶ στεφάνη τριχῶν.

SACERDOS

The only priestess appearing among the Dramatis Personae is in the Rudens — Ptolemocratia Sacerdos Veneris. Greeted as *mater* (263; cf. 289) by the shipwrecked Palaestra and Ampelisca, she returns their salutation with *salvete, puellae.* Embracing her knees they beg for pity and assistance (274–280). No hint is given concerning her costume, but from Pollux (Onom. IV, 119) we learn what its colour probably was: Ἡ δὲ γυναικῶν ἐσθὴς κωμικῶν, ἡ μὲν τῶν γραῶν μηλίνη ἢ ἀερίνη, πλὴν ἱερειῶν. ταύταις δὲ λευκή.

SYCOPHANTA

This rôle is found twice in Plautus (Ps. and Tri.), but not at all in Terence.

(1) Simia Sycophanta is a slave from Carystos, in regard to whom Pseudolus, replying to the question *Qua facie?* says *Malum, callidum, doctum,* etc. (Ps. 724–727). He is disguised for the pur-

poses of the plot as a foreigner,[1] a soldier's servus, *i.e.*, as Harpax Cacula (see CACULA, pp. 115–117). He wears a long-sleeved tunic, a *chlamys*, and a *petasus*, and carries a *machaera* (735, 738, 756–757, 963–964). His haughty bearing (911, 917–918) may have been required by his rôle.

(2) The Sycophanta of the Trinummus is apparently not a slave (815); because of the plot he is also disguised as a foreigner (767–768, 840).[1] He probably wore a *chlamys*, and his hat seems to have been very big (851–852). He is a trickster who hopes to cheat even the man who hired him out of the garments rented from the *choragus* (857–859).[2] His character shows in his face.

Lorenz's objection to *adulescens* as applied to a Cacula, a Danista, a Parasitus, has already been mentioned (pp. 116, n. 1; 119; 87); in the same class he includes[3] the Sycophanta. Both of our Sycophantae are addressed as *adulescentes* (Ps. 978; Tri. 871, 889, 892, 968). Under CACULA, I questioned the reasonableness of Lorenz's objection in the case of Harpax; therefore, since Simia is counterfeiting Harpax, we cannot accept his objection to the epithet as applied to Simia. There is no inherent reason why a Sycophanta should not be young.

---

[1] Cf. p. 83, n. 1. [2] See p. 18.
[3] See Lorenz's note on Mo. 653.

### TIBICEN

In two plays — the Casina and the Stichus — a Tibicen is among the Dramatis Personae, but in both cases he is a *persona muta*.

In the Casina, the Tibicen is exhorted to play a hymeneal song while the bride is being led out (798–799). In the Stichus, the Tibicen is present at a banquet and alternately pipes and drinks (715 ff.); he has his *tibiae* (718, 723–724, 767).

Wieseler (Taf. IV, 10) reproduces an ancient relief showing a tragic actor in the costume of Dionysus, turning his face towards a woman, while close beside him stands a boy playing a flute. In connection with this relief and Tafel XI, 1, in which a maiden is playing double pipes, Wieseler remarks (p. 82 b) that neither flute-player is full grown. The boy wears no *chiton*, only a scant mantle.

Cf. also the flute-player on a vase by Brygos (Taf. 50, representing a κῶμος, Furtwängler u. Reichhold, Series I, München, 1900). The flute-player wears a crown ornamented with leaves.

### TIBICINA

In the Epidicus two Tibicinae, Phrygia and Eleusium, are among the Dramatis Personae. They are hired for a wedding celebration and are only *personae mutae.* Probably they had their *tibiae* with them (cf. FIDICINA, pp. 126–127).

Wieseler (Taf. XI, 1) reproduces an ancient relief from the Museo Borbonico, depicting a most interesting scene from the stage. On the right a young man and a slave are engaged in some sort of struggle, which two old men on the left are excitedly discussing; in the centre a maiden [1] plays the double pipes. She wears a long, loose undergarment, low-necked and sleeveless, and her mantle has fallen to her hips and is knotted together in front.

Cf. a flute-player on a vase by Brygos (Taf. 50, representing a κῶμος, Furtwängler u. Reichhold, Series I, München, 1900). The woman wears a long scarf bound crown-like about her head, with the long ends hanging down behind.

## TONSTRIX

Archilis Tonstrix, who has been employed by Phronesium Meretrix to help carry out the deception practised on Stratophanes Miles, is an *ancilla* (Tru. 771). She is suspected by Callicles Senex and, with another *ancilla*, her accomplice, is bound (Tru. 771, 783–784, 837–838) and made

---

[1] Cf. Wieseler's comment on the age of flute-players, under TIBICEN (p. 138).

to confess the truth. No hint is given of her costume (see ANCILLA, pp. 52–55, for probable costume).

### TRAPEZITA

This rôle occurs but once in Plautus and not at all in Terence (cf. DANISTA, p. 118).

Lyco is the greedy Trapezita of the Curculio. We have only one line descriptive of his appearance (389):

> Quis hic est qui *operto capite* Aesculapium
> salutat?

This line, has, however, no significance in connection with him as a Trapezita, for it merely describes a man in an act of worship (cf. Verg. Aen. 3. 405).[1]

### VILICUS

This rôle is found twice in Plautus[2] and not at all in Terence.

There is a considerable amount of description of Olympio Vilicus, who is a slave in the Casina. At verse 446 we read of him:

> At *candidatus* cedit hic mastigia
> stimulorum loculi,

but this, as most of the references, deals with his

---

[1] We have here, then, a Roman touch in Plautus. See Conington's note on Vergil, *l.c.*

[2] In the Casina and the Poenulus.

appearance when dressed as a bridegroom; cf. lines 767 ff.,

> Vilicus is autem *cum corona candide*
> *vestitus lautus exornatusque* ambulat,

and 796 (cf. 934):

> Sed eccum progreditur *cum corona et lampade.*

In a very corrupt scene we get a possible reference to his beard, and at the end of the scene, where the text is much better, we hear that he has lost his *palliolum* (934) and gotten bruised in an encounter of which Casina was the apparent cause. For the value of *hoc ornatu* (932) see p. 23.

Again, in the case of Collabiscus Vilicus our information is concerning his disguise as a Spartan (Poe. 770, 780) soldier (801–802) — a *peregrinus* (600, 649 ff., 656, 675).[1] He is *basilice exornatus* (577; cf. 425–426), is *chlamydatus* (620, 644), and has three hundred *nummi* (594, 714–715), which would imply a *crumina* or a *marsuppium.* Especially interesting is his use of the *aurum comicum,* or stage-money, consisting of lupines (Poe. 597–598):[2]

> *Aurumst* profecto hic, spectatores, *comicum:*
> macerato hoc pingues fiunt auro in barbaria boves.

---

[1] See p. 83, n. 1.

[2] For discussion see Class. Rev. 17, 160 ff., A Roman Stage Convention, by R. H. Malden.

## BIBLIOGRAPHY

I have had access to the following works which contain reproductions of the illustrations from the MSS. of Terence:


Seroux d'Agincourt, Histoire de l'art par les monuments. Paris, 1823. Vol. V, plates 35 and 36, contains seven pictures from C.

Champollion, Paléographie des Classiques latins. Paris, 1837. Plate IV contains the picture for Eun. II, 2 from P.

Silvestre, Paléographie universelle. Paris, 1841. Contains one picture from Parisinus 7899 and two from C.

Wieseler, Theatergebäude und Denkmäler des Bühnenwesens bei den Griechen und Römern. Göttingen, 1851. Plate X contains six pictures from C and one from F; there is explanatory text on pp. 63–81.

Chatelain, Paléographie des Classiques latins. Paris, 1884–1892. I. Plate VII contains two pictures from P and one from F.

Baumeister, Denkmäler des klassischen Altertums. München u. Leipzig, 1884. In the article entitled Lustspiel are two pictures from C.

Morgan and Greenough's Phormio. Harvard University, Cambridge, 1900. Contains photographic reproductions of all the pictures of the Phormio from C.

Terenti Codex Ambrosianus H 75 inf. phototypice editus. Praefatus est Ericus Bethe. Accedunt 91 imagines ex aliis Terenti codicibus et libris impressis nunc primum collectae et editae. Lugduni Batavorum, 1903. A. W. Sijthoff.

Karl E. Weston, The Illustrated Terence Manuscripts, with drawings of all the pictures of the Phormio extant in C, P, F, and O. Harvard Studies, 14 (1903).

Album Terentianum picturas continens ex imagine phototypa Lugdunensi Terenti codd. Ambrosiani H 75 inf. et Parisini 7899 sumptas et lithographice expressas. Praefatus et picturas Latine interpretatus est Iacobus van Wageningen. Groningen, 1907. Noordhoff.

Among the discussions bearing on the general subject of the illustrated MSS. of Terence and not included in the above volumes, the following have been especially useful:

Leo, Die Ueberlieferungsgeschichte der terenzischen Komödien und der Kommentar des Donatus, Rheinisches Museum, 38 (1883), pp. 317–347.

Sittl, Die Gebärden der Griechen u. Römer. Leipzig, 1890.

Basore, The Scenic Value of the Miniatures in the Manuscripts of Terence. Studies in honour of B. L. Gildersleeve. Baltimore, 1902.

Engelhardt, Die Illustrationen der Terenzhandschriften. Ein Beitrag zur Geschichte des Buchschmucks. Jena, 1905.

Many manuals which treat of Roman life in general contain valuable detailed discussions of the Greek and

Roman theatre. Among such discussions special mention should be made of:

Die griechischen Bühnenaltertümer, by Dr. Albert Müller, in Hermann's Lehrbuch der griechischen Antiquitäten, III, 2. Freiburg, 1886.

Das Bühnenwesen der Griechen u. Römer, by Dr. Gustav Oehmichen. Iwan Müller's Handbuch, V, 3. B. München, 1890.

Of special interest in studying the costume of the Roman Prologus is Les Prologues de Térence, by Philippe Fabia, Paris, 1888.

For a comparison of the miniatures of the Terence MSS. with other artistic remains the following works are especially important:

Helbig, Wandgemälde der vom Vesuv verschütteten Städte Campaniens. Leipzig, 1868.

Wilpert, Die Malereien der Katakomben Roms. Mit 267 Tafeln u. 54 Abbildungen im Text. Freiburg, 1903.

Springer's Handbuch der Kunstgeschichte. Das Mittelalter, $II^7$. Leipzig, 1904.